BURNING WOOD AND COAL

by
Susan MacKay
L. Dale Baker
John W. Bartok, Jr.
James P. Lassoie

NORTHEAST REGIONAL AGRICULTURAL ENGINEERING SERVICE

ITHACA, NEW YORK 14853

Publication Number: NRAES-23

Library of Congress Cataloging-in-Publication
Data
Burning wood and coal.
    (Publication ; no. NRAES-23)
    Rev and updated version of: Burning wood,
1977, and Burning coal, 1978.
    Bibliography: p.
    1. Wood as fuel. 2. Coal. I. MacKay, Susan,
1944—   . II. Burning wood. III. Burning
coal IV. Series: Publication (Northeast Regional
Agricultural Engineering Service) ; NRAES-23.
TP324.B87   1985   697'.042   85-25966
ISBN 0-935817-00-X

AUTHORS

Susan MacKay, Northeast Regional Agricultural Engineering Service

L. Dale Baker, International Harvester, Chicago, IL

John W. Bartok, Jr., Dept. of Agricultural Engineering, Univ. of Connecticut

J.P. Lassoie, Dept. of Natural Resources, Cornell University

ACKNOWLEDGEMENTS

This book is a revised and updated version of *Burning Wood* and *Burning Coal*, published by the Northeast Regional Agricultural Engineering Service. The authors wish to thank the following people for their contributions to the original *Burning Wood*.

W.D. Lilley, College of Forest Resources, University of Maine

E.L. Palmer, Dept. of Agricultural Engineering, U. of Connecticut

D.W. Taber, Dept. of Natural Resources, Cornell University

and S.A. Weeks, Agway, Inc., Syracuse

The Northeast Regional Agricultural Engineering Service (NRAES) is an activity of the Cooperative Extension Services of the Northeast Land Grant Universities and the United States Department of Agriculture. Headquarters are located at Riley Robb Hall, Cornell University, Ithaca, New York 14853. (607) 256-7654

The following are cooperating members:

University of Connecticut
University of Delaware
University of Maine
University of Maryland
University of Massachusetts
University of New Hampshire
Rutgers University
Cornell University
Pennsylvania State University
University of Rhode Island
University of Vermont
West Virginia University
University of the District of Columbia

CONTENTS

I—The Solid Fuels: Evaluating Options

In the mid-nineteenth century, wood met about 90% of the fuel needs of the United States. A century later, coal provided more heat for commercial and residential use in the U. S. than all other fuels combined. As heating oil became inexpensive in the late 1940's, coal was gradually replaced by oil and natural gas because of their competitive cost, greater convenience and cleaner-burning qualities. With the decline of domestic oil and natural gas reserves and the continuing price increases for foreign oil, interest in wood burning for home heating had a strong revival in the 1970's. Coincident with this was a modest revival in coal-burning for home heating. In the last 10 years, major advances in stove design have caught up with present day sophisticated demands for convenience, while at the same time reducing creosote and emission problems, resulting in more efficient burning of solid fuels.

Purchasing any new heating system is costly, but solid fuel systems, in addition, require a change in life style. It is important to analyze your needs and be aware of both the cost of the equipment and long term costs. This booklet provides an overview of the state-of-the-art of solid fuel burning. It offers the pros and cons of wood and coal as fuels, helps you evaluate your needs and decide on available equipment options, gives specifics on stove installation, operation and maintenance tips. Appendices give detailed information about purchasing and storing coal and about harvesting, seasoning, and storing wood.

THE SOLID FUELS

Wood and coal may always be somewhat less expensive than natural gas, oil and electricity because they are less convenient and do not provide as even and controllable heat output. Solid fuels involve a daily commitment of labor and attention - to store and handle the fuel, tend the fire and remove the ashes.

Both wood and coal (particularly coal) are difficult to burn efficiently at the beginning and end of winter, without overheating the house. Solid fuels cannot be fully automated, so without a backup heat system they present the risk of frozen pipes and costly repairs. For these reasons they are often used to supplement an existing system using oil, gas, or electricity.

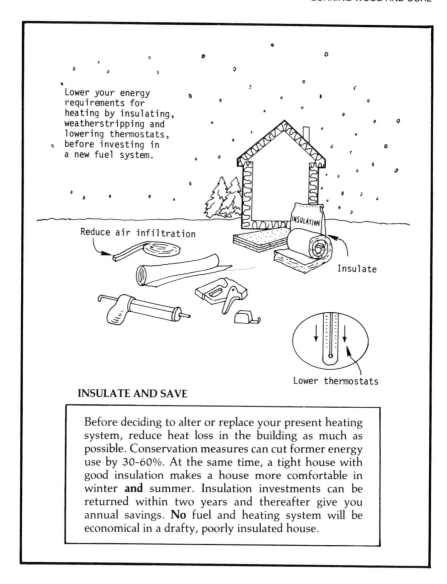

Lower your energy requirements for heating by insulating, weatherstripping and lowering thermostats, before investing in a new fuel system.

Reduce air infiltration

Insulate

Lower thermostats

INSULATE AND SAVE

Before deciding to alter or replace your present heating system, reduce heat loss in the building as much as possible. Conservation measures can cut former energy use by 30-60%. At the same time, a tight house with good insulation makes a house more comfortable in winter **and** summer. Insulation investments can be returned within two years and thereafter give you annual savings. **No** fuel and heating system will be economical in a drafty, poorly insulated house.

Safety and automated combustion features which are part of oil and gas furnaces allow you to set the thermostat and forget it. With coal or wood burning stoves, a much greater awareness of fuel characteristics and combustion techniques is required to use the fuel efficiently and safely, and to prevent the emission of large quantities of pollutants into the air. This problem has been overcome to an extent with some of the newer wood stove designs and catalytic combustors. Coal furnaces or boilers with stokers can be almost completely automated, making the heating system almost as easy to operate as with oil or natural gas furnaces.

Wood or Coal?

Wood is more readily available outside of urban areas. But even in rural areas, wood, that was once almost free except for labor, is now becoming expensive and more difficult to obtain. It is important to shop around and arrange for a reliable wood supply, since there are so many variables in wood (type of wood, amount of moisture, amount of labor to get it fire-ready, etc.) and in its measurement (cord, face cord, truckload, etc.). Experienced wood burners in your area can often suggest excellent sources of firewood and steer you clear of sources where they have been "burned."

Figure 1. Comparing Wood and Coal

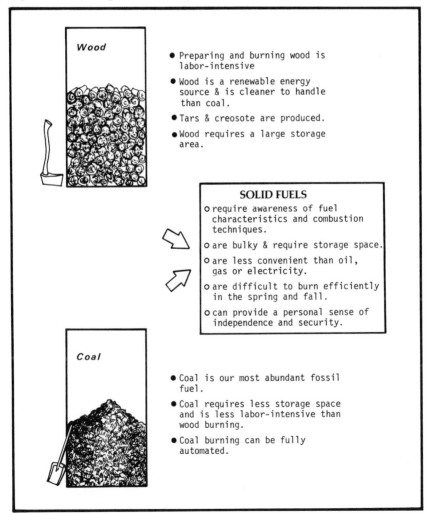

Wood

- Preparing and burning wood is labor-intensive
- Wood is a renewable energy source & is cleaner to handle than coal.
- Tars & creosote are produced.
- Wood requires a large storage area.

SOLID FUELS

o require awareness of fuel characteristics and combustion techniques.

o are bulky & require storage space.

o are less convenient than oil, gas or electricity.

o are difficult to burn efficiently in the spring and fall.

o can provide a personal sense of independence and security.

Coal

- Coal is our most abundant fossil fuel.
- Coal requires less storage space and is less labor-intensive than wood burning.
- Coal burning can be fully automated.

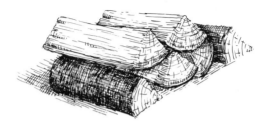

If you own, or have access to a woodlot, consider your time or cost to prepare the wood for fuel. Cutting, hauling and stacking your own wood supply is hard work, time-consuming and potentially dangerous. On the other hand, some people find the physical exercise, the shared family responsibility, and sense of independence relaxing and enjoyable.

The moisture content of freshly cut wood can be as high as 60%, so wood must be cut in advance and properly seasoned. It is relatively bulky for the amount of heat derived, compared to coal or oil, so a large, covered storage area is needed. Stove pipes and chimneys need periodic cleaning to remove soot and creosote.

Wood is relative easy to ignite and burn, so stove designs have been relatively simple. But in the past 10 years many advances have been made in wood stove design to get the most heat from the fuel and to reduce creosote and emission problems. The most dramatic and accessible of these changes is the catalytic combustor stove.

Coal, while not renewable, represents approximately 85% of the U.S. fossil fuel reserves. Anthracite, the preferred coal for home heating, is available in most parts of the Northeast. The revival of coal-burning is not yet as widespread as the revival of wood-burning. It is generally turned to for practical reasons such as its hard to beat cost, its compactness and its lower labor requirements.

The moisture content of coal is much lower than wood, so less heat is wasted to drive off moisture. In addition, creosote does not form during combustion of hard coal. But the kindling temperature of coal (750-975°F) is much higher than wood (550°F), so that coal fires are more difficult to start, and more heat must be maintained within the fuel bed to keep the fire burning. Stove design requirements are more elaborate than for wood, so the stove itself will cost more than the average wood stove.

Coal is also dirtier to handle and burn than wood. You can expect to have more dust in the house, especially if the stove is located in the living area. Coal ashes are 7-10 times more abundant than wood ashes and are laden with chemical compounds that may be harmful to the soil; disposal of ashes, then, becomes a regular chore. Fly ash and soot in the chimney also means regular chimney cleaning to maintain the strong draft necessary for coal burning.

On the other hand, coal is more compact, requiring about one third the storage space of wood with an equivalent heat value. Coal fires also have a more even heat output than wood. Coal is less labor-intensive; the fire can be maintained for longer periods than wood, without loss of efficiency and potentially dangerous creosote formation. Coal furnaces and boilers can also be more fully automated for fuel loading and ash removal than their wood counterparts. Another advantage of the coal stove or heater is that it can be used to burn both coal and wood, whereas a wood burning unit can only be used for wood.

COMPARING HEATING FUEL COSTS

The costs of various forms of energy are evaluated in different ways, making comparisons difficult. Figure 2 will enable you to compare the market value of various heating fuels on the basis of their heating equivalent as expressed in dollars per million British thermal units[1] ($/MBtu). Heater efficiencies are included in the figure.

To use the chart, determine the local market value of the fuel you wish to compare, and read across the fuel price columns to the Heating Equivalent column to determine the price per MBtu.

For example, if anthracite coal is available for $120 per ton, the heating equivalent cost is approximately $8.00/MBtu. Fuel oil at $1.10/gallon has a heating equivalent cost of $10.60/MBtu. In this case, it may pay to switch tc coal because the cost of coal is significantly less than the cost of oil.

---

[1]A Btu (British thermal unit) is the amount of heat required to heat one pound (a pint) of water one degree Fahrenheit.

Figure 2.Comparing Heating Fuel Costs

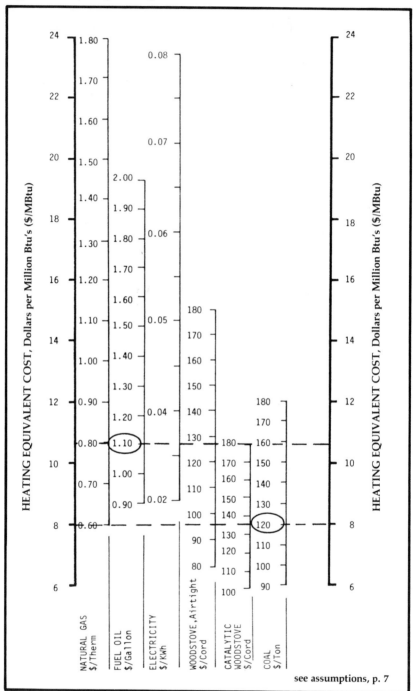

see assumptions, p. 7

CONVERSION TO A SOLID FUEL

It is important to realize the total costs of converting the typical home to supplemental wood or coal heating. Many economic comparisons consider only relative fuel costs and neglect the expenses of purchasing, installing, and maintaining an additional heating unit. For those cutting their own wood, there are equipment costs and personal time involved. At $5 per hour, a winter's supply of firewood may be worth about $650 in an individual's time. Those considering conversion must be ready for a change in lifestyle. To many, working up a fuel supply and tending a woodstove are enjoyable activities; to others this is just hard work which detracts from other activities. Those who do convert are making a long term commitment to paying more attention to their heating needs.

Before purchasing a new solid fuel system, first decide how it will be used. Consider the total cost of installing a stove. Remember you may need to buy stove pipe, floor and wall protection and a chimney as well as accessories. A complete installation can cost a thousand dollars and up which will take many years to pay back. Often this money is better spent on insulating and weatherizing the house before switching fuels.

A knowledge of combustion basics and commonly used solid fuel terms will help you evaluate the options presented in the following chapters on fireplaces, stoves and central heating systems.

ASSUMPTIONS

```
NATURAL GAS —   Therm = 100,000 Btu = approx. 100 cu ft.
                75% Efficiency.  $/MBtu = 13.33 x $/Therm

FUEL OIL — 138,000 Btu/Gallon.
                75% Efficiency.  $/MBtu = 9.66 x $/Gallon

ELECTRICITY — 3412 Btu/kWh.
                100% Efficiency.  $/MBtu = 293 x $/kWh

MIXED HARDWOODS — 24MBtu/Cord. 'Airtight' Stove - 50% Efficiency.
                                $/MBtu = $/Cord/12
                                Catalytic Woodstove - 70% Efficiency.
                                $/MBtu = $/Cord/17

COAL - 12,500 Btu/lb.
        60% Efficiency. $/MBtu = $/ton/15
```

COMBUSTION BASICS

The combustion of wood and coal involves the mixing of carbon and hydrogen from the fuels with oxygen from the air to form carbon dioxide, water and heat. Combustion has three requirements-fuel, air, and heat. If any of these three are removed, burning ceases. When all three are available in the correct proportion, combustion is self-sustaining because the fuel releases more than enough heat to initiate further burning.

The rate at which wood or coal burns is controlled by the amount of air available. Little or no air causes wood to smolder and produce pollutants or it stops combustion. Too much air will cool the fire, remove the heat, and essentially blow the fire out.

Another important aspect of combustion is the energy content of the fuel. Energy content is a measure of the available chemical energy per pound and is normally expressed in British thermal units (Btu's). Heating value is the amount of heat actually available from a fuel. Heating value will be directly related to the energy content but other factors, such as moisture content of the fuel, also affect, the heating value. Table 1 shows heating values for several common fuels.

Table 1. Heating Value of Common Fuels

TYPE of FUEL	BRITISH THERMAL UNITS (Btu)/POUND
Wood, 50% moisture	Approximately 4,700
Wood, 20% moisture	Approximately 6,200
Coal	11,000 - 14,000
#2 Fuel Oil	19,700
Natural Gas	22,800

COMBUSTION of WOOD

Combustion transforms wood into heat, chemicals, and gases by chemical combination of hydrogen and carbon in the fuel with oxygen in the air. Complete combustion produces water vapor and carbon dioxide along with heat and noncombustible ashes. When incomplete combustion occurs, carbon monoxide, hydrocarbons, and other gases are formed. Figure 3 illustrates the stages of wood combustion.

Figure 3. Combustion of Wood

FIRST STAGE 	The wood is heated to evaporate and drive off moisture. This heat does not warm the stove or room.
SECOND STAGE 500°F - 1100°F 	The wood starts to break down chemically at 500°F and volatile matter is vaporized. These vapors contain between 50-60% of the heat value of the wood. At 1100°F these vapors burn. This high temperature must be maintained for maximum efficiency of combustion.
THIRD STAGE over 1100°F 	Following the release of volatile gases, the remaining material (charcoal) burns at temperatures exceeding 1100°F.

Approximately 50-60% of the heat available from burning wood is in the volatile gases. All three phases of burning may occur at the same time. However, the first two phases usually occur when the fire is started or when wood is added. For efficient burning, the volatiles must be mixed with air and kept at a high enough temperature to burn completely inside the heating unit.

Wood varies in size, density and moisture content; it is not a simple, uniform fuel like natural gas, propane or fuel oil. Gas and oil can be burned at fairly high efficiencies because the burner always operates at full output, and the fuel can easily be started and stopped. Wood-fueled heaters operate most efficiently when they are burning at high temperatures.

In spring and fall it is difficult to operate wood stoves at full output to create high enough temperatures for good combustion without overheating the room. If the stove is normally operated at reduced draft in order to achieve a comfortable room temperature, or in order to hold the fire overnight, the efficiency of the stove is decreased.

COMBUSTION of COAL

The combustible portions of coal are fixed carbon, volatile matter (gaseous compounds of hydrogen and carbon) and small amounts of sulfur. Before a material will ignite with oxygen, its kindling temperature must be reached. The kindling temperature occurs when a fuel starts to change from its solid state to a combustible gas.

This temperature varies with different materials, as shown in Table 2. Complete combustion means burning all the gases and all of the carbon or solid portion of the fuel that is possible under ordinary conditions. Figure 4 illustrates the basic principles of coal combustion.

Table 2. Kindling Temperatures of Various Fuels

FUEL	KINDLING TEMPERATURE, °F
Wood	550
Soft Charcoal	650
Cannel Coal	668
High Volatile Bituminous	765
Low Volatile Bituminous	870
Anthracite	925
Hydrogen	1,031-1,130
Carbon Monoxide	1,200-1,292
Methane	1,202
Sulfur	470

[1]The kindling temperature occurs when a fuel starts to change from its solid state to a combustible gas.

When coal starts to burn, volatile matter is driven off. This may take only a few minutes with anthracite, slightly longer with low-volatile bituminous, or 10 to 15 minutes with softer coals. Volatile matter does not exist in coal, as such, but it is produced by the decomposition of coal when heated. It consists chiefly of the combustible gases - hydrogen, carbon monoxide, methane and other hydrocarbons, tar vapors, volatile sulfur compounds and some noncombustible gases such as carbon dioxide and water vapor.

Ignition of the volatiles takes place above the fuelbed. It requires a high enough temperature for the gases to ignite and a sufficient quantity of oxygen to complete their combustion.

Figure 4. Combustion of Coal

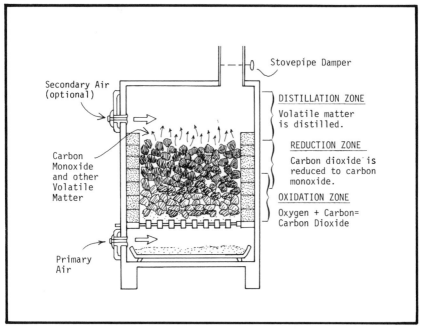

EFFICIENCY

Efficiency is the percentage or fraction of chemical energy available from the fuel that heats the room. Efficiency depends on the fuel used, the skill of the operator, and the design of the stove and chimney.

For a stove to have high overall energy efficiency it must perform two jobs well. First, the fuel must be burned as completely as possible so very little smoke goes out the chimney (combustion efficiency). Second, the stove must transfer the heat in the stove to the room (heat transfer efficiency).

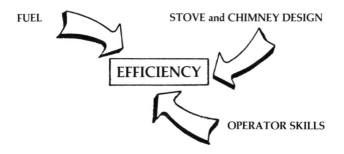

Increased heater efficiency has been a major concern of most solid fuel manufacturers. In addition to burning less fuel for a given amount of heat, efficient stoves produce fewer emissions and creosote. However, the lack of consistent rating methods among manufacturers makes comparisons difficult for the consumer. Table 3 shows the range of energy efficiencies you can expect from various types of available solid fuel burners.

Table 3. Energy Efficiency for Various Heating Units

TYPE of HEATING UNIT	EFFICIENCY RANGE
Masonry, Manufactured or Freestanding Fireplace	-10% - 20%
Fireplace with Heat Exchanger and outside combustion air	10% - 30%
Modular Concrete Heat-storing Fireplace	35% - 40%
Fireplace with 'Airtight' Stove Insert	35% - 50%
'Airtight' Stove	45% - 50%
'Airtight' Stove with Add-on Catalytic Converter	55% - 70%
Catalytic Stove	65% - 75%
Wood Furnace	50% - 70%
Gas or Oil-fired Furnace	65% - 85%
Electrical Heat	100%

POLLUTION and AIR QUALITY

Widespread residential use of solid fuels could threaten air quality. Wood smoke contains, among other things, carbon monoxide, nitrogen oxides, methane, formadelhyde and particulates or solid unburned hydrocarbons. Incomplete combustion of coal can release carbon monoxide, other volatile gases and particles of carbon into the atmosphere. Burning anthracite is essentially much cleaner than wood in terms of potential for atmospheric pollution; it has a very low sulfur content. Soft coal, particularly high-volatile bituminous coal, has much greater potential for pollution than anthracite, which usually contains less than 8% volatile matter. (Figure 5)

Figure 5. Potentially Dangerous Emissions from Solid Fuels

COMPARING FUEL EMISSIONS[1]

1. Low levels of particulate matter and carbon monoxide are emitted with combustion of #2 Fuel oil.

2. Hard coal is slightly dirtier than #2 Fuel oil and emits much more carbon monoxide than #2 Fuel oil.

3. Wood, wood pellets and soft coal produce 60 times the amount of particulate matter emissions and 300 times more carbon monoxide than a comparable (energy wise) amount of # 2 Fuel oil.

[1]Adapted from findings in a study by S. Butcher, Prof. of Chemistry, Bowdoin College, published by the Maine Dept. of Human Services. 1983

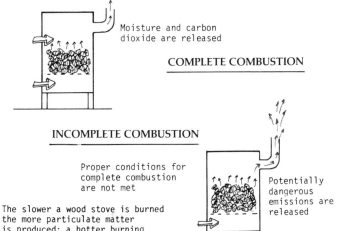

Moisture and carbon dioxide are released

COMPLETE COMBUSTION

INCOMPLETE COMBUSTION

Proper conditions for complete combustion are not met

The slower a wood stove is burned the more particulate matter is produced; a hotter burning stove will burn cleaner

Potentially dangerous emissions are released

PARTICULATE MATTER (Soot) - Particulates produce pollution which reduces visibility, smells bad and reduces heating system efficiency.

1. LARGE AIRBORNE PARTICLES of carbon can be caught in the nostrils and upper respiratory system.

2. TINIER AIRBORNE PARTICLES of carbon are more dangerous, since they lodge in the lungs and can aggravate respiratory problems such as broncitis, emphysema, asthma and tuberculosis.

VOLATILE MATTER

3. CARBON MONOXIDE formed by incomplete combustion of carbon is odorless, colorless and tasteless. Air containing only 1/2 of 1% of carbon monoxide would, after sufficient time, cause death.

4. NITROUS OXIDES contribute to smog formation.

5. SULFUR OXIDES. Sulfur combines with oxygen to form sulfur dioxide. It then reacts with moisture and oxygen in the atmosphere to produce an airborne sulfuric acid, which is harmful to humans and vegetation, as well as corrosive to metals and mortar.

Certain meteorological conditions, such as severe temperature inversions, aggravate problems associated with stove emissions. In this condition, an upper layer of warm air traps a lower layer of colder air and smoke, reducing visibility and creating health hazards (Figure 6). In some areas, notably Montana, Oregon and Colorado, communities with recurrent air pollution problems have restricted the types of wood stoves homeowners can install or they have imposed stringent fines for burning wood when air-monitoring devices indicate high pollution levels.

Figure 6. Pollution Problems can be Aggravated by Weather and Geographic Conditions.

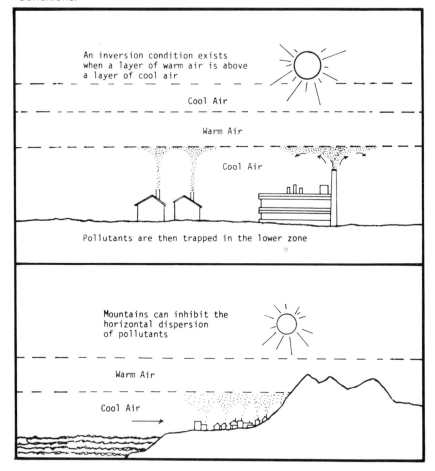

Most wood smoke problems which occur are not due to the nature of the fuel so much as the manner of operation. Under conditions of low heat demand, people adjust controlled combustion wood stoves to restrict the airflow to the firebox and produce a slow-burning, air-starved fire. This practice produces comfortable levels of heat and a long burn, but also volumes of smoke. Much of the heat potential goes up the chimney as smoke, which forms creosote deposits (necessitating costly chimney cleaning and producing a fire hazard) and pollutes the air.

New-technology stoves and retrofit devices have been developed to counteract these problems and to produce relatively clean exhausts by burning the wood smoke itself. Benefits include more heat for the fuel dollar, reduction in creosote deposits, and improved air quality.

II—Fireplaces

A **masonry fireplace** supplies radiant energy to bring quick comfort to a cold room. However, it is a very inefficient heater. In addition, air that supports combustion in the fireplace is drawn from the room, and must be replaced by cold outside air. **The heat radiated to the room may be less than the heat contained in the air that is drawn up the chimney.** Additional heat can be lost if the flue damper is left open after the fire dies out.

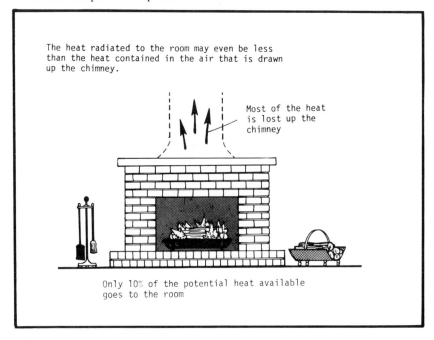

The heat radiated to the room may even be less than the heat contained in the air that is drawn up the chimney.

Most of the heat is lost up the chimney

Only 10% of the potential heat available goes to the room

Factory-built fireplaces, sometimes called zero clearance fireplaces, may be installed in direct contact with combustible walls. Other **metal free standing fireplaces** must be placed out in the room at least 36″ away from unprotected combustible walls. These metal fireplaces have about the same efficiency as masonry fireplaces, but they warm up faster. Of course, they cool rapidly once the fire dies down.

Figure 7. Fireplace Options

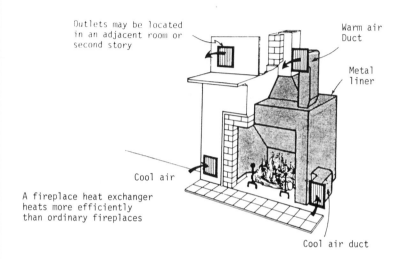

HEAT EXCHANGER

Outlets may be located
in an adjacent room or
second story

Warm air
Duct

Metal
liner

Cool air

A fireplace heat exchanger
heats more efficiently
than ordinary fireplaces

Cool air duct

GLASS DOORS

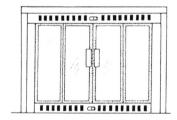

Glass doors reduce the amount of warm air from
the room that is lost up the chimney.

STOVE INSERTS

The fireplace can be converted to an efficient
heater with a solid fuel controlled combustion insert.

At the time of construction, a **fireplace heat exchanger** can be installed in a masonry fireplace to circulate air from the room behind the metal fire box and out into the room either along the edge or above the fireplace mantle. A fan can be placed in the duct in some of these units. A heat exchanger can double the heat that reaches the room from a conventional fireplace.

Some new fireplace designs featuring **heat-storing modular concrete,** have been tested in independent laboratories at 35-40% overall efficiency and 95% combustion efficiency. This type of fireplace works on the principle of a hot, brisk fire generating high temperatures that warm a large thermal mass (concrete). The mass then radiates into the room to provide heat after the fire burns. The hot fires burn clean, emit very low levels of particulates into the air and cause little creosote build-up.

Tubes or hollow grates are available that can be placed in the fireplace to provide additional heat by air circulation. Some of these units rely on natural airflow, others use a fan. Recent tests have proven them to be of little value.

Tight fitting **glass doors** on the fireplace greatly reduce the radiation that reaches the room. However, the doors also reduce the amount of warm air from the room that is lost up the chimney. Probably the most heat will be gained if the doors are opened during the hotter stages of the fire and closed as the fire dies out. The greatest savings occur when the closed doors control the loss of heat overnight. A tight fitting metal door could also be used.

Many **fireplace stove inserts** have been developed that fit inside and increase the efficiency of the fireplace. They are available in a wide range of styles for both wood and coal. They may be constructed with heavy plate steel, have fire brick liners, and contain double or triple walls with a fan. Their main advantage is that inserts do not require installing a new chimney or rearranging the living space. Their disadvantage is that there is really no good way to clean the chimney without removing the heavy insert. Some weigh 400 pounds or more.

Before buying an insert, carefully measure the fireplace width, height and depth to be sure the insert will fit. Then follow the manufacturer's instructions for installation. In a typical installation the original damper is removed and replaced with a metal flue plate. Be sure the steel cover panels that close off the space between the insert and the fireplace opening form a good seal. Use furnace cement or fiberglass and high temperature silicon sealant to seal gaps between bricks or large stoves and the cover.

A stove may also be set in front of a fireplace and connected to the existing chimney. There are several ways to insert the stovepipe into the chimney. One way is to remove the damper and insert the stove pipe through a snug fitting metal sheet placed in the damper opening. Be sure the stove pipe can easily be removed for cleaning. (Figure 8)

If the stove is too tall for the stove pipe to be inserted directly into the fireplace, the connection can be made above the fireplace. A thimble may have to be

Figure 8. Installing a Stove in Front of a Fireplace

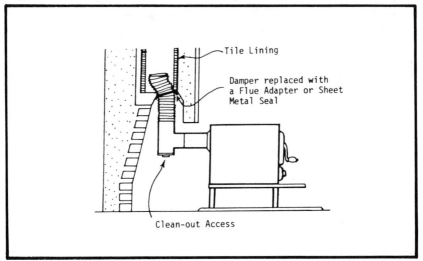

installed. This connection requires cutting or breaking the tile flue liner and is not easy to do. Hire a qualified mason for this job. Be sure proper clearances to combustibles are kept.

In some instances creosote may run down toward the fireplace past the damper and accumulate in the original fireplace opening. Check frequently for creosote accumulation.

III—Stoves

There are thousands of manufacturers of stoves throughout the world. Size, appearance, style, finish, construction, materials, weight, durability, and ability to burn the fuel efficiently for maximum heat are just some of the characteristics to be evaluated.

STOVE SIZE

There is no simple, consistent method to rate stove heating capacity. Various methods include the number of cubic feet the unit will heat, the heat output in Btu's or the amount of fuel the stove will hold.

Factors which influence the size of the stove needed are:
- Severity of the weather conditions
- Particular conditions of the area to be heated, including the weather tightness of the home and the configurations of the rooms and passages to be heated.
- Type of fuel used
- Function. Is the stove the primary heat source, or is there a backup heat source?

Oversizing is the most common and serious problem. Not only is there a higher initial cost, but it will be diffiult to burn the fuel efficiently without overheating, particularly during the fall and spring. If the stove is sized for **average** winter use, rather than for the coldest possible conditions, it will be easier to maintain the fire and to burn the fuel efficiently. If there is an adequate backup heat source, a moderately undersized stove is better yet. A local, established stove dealer should have the best experience to help you select the right size for the area you want to heat.

MATERIALS OF CONSTRUCTION

Sheet metal stoves of relatively thin gauge have been used for many years for heating. They are relatively inexpensive but have a shorter life than plate steel or cast iron stoves. They will quickly heat a room, but they also cool rapidly when the fire dies down. If occasional quick heating is needed, such as for a cabin or emergency use, thin walled stoves are appropriate.

Plate steel stoves made from steel 1/8″ or thicker are also available. These welded stoves hold heat longer than sheet metal stoves. Many of these stoves are lined with firebrick to protect the metal and to provide more even heat.

Cast iron stoves hold up well under heat, have a long life, spread the heat away from hot spots in the fire, and generally do not warp. They crack easily if dropped. Have used cast iron stoves thoroughly inspected by persons knowledgeable in their construction to determine if there are any cracked, broken, or missing parts, or areas that are warped or thin.

Soapstone, an attractive, soft stone composed essentially of talc, is used as decoration and the walls for some stoves. Because it has about twice the heat holding capacity of steel it provides even heat over a long period.

STOVE TYPES

Most wood and coal stoves transfer heat to the room by radiating heat from the hot surface of the stove. **Radiant heaters** produce heat that is most intense at close proximity and diminishes rapidly with distance from the stove. Surfaces in direct line with the stove will be heated. Many people find the comfort of radiant heat hard to beat and enjoy the fact that family activities tend to center around the fire.(Figure 9)

Circulating stoves are constructed with a metal box spaced about one inch from the wall of the firebox. Vents in the top and bottom of the outer box allow natural air currents to carry the heat away from the stove. The outer surface of a circulating stove is not as hot as a radiant stove and thus can be installed closer to combustible material than radiant stoves. Circulating stoves are better suited to heating a large room than radiant stoves.

Figure 9. Types of Stoves

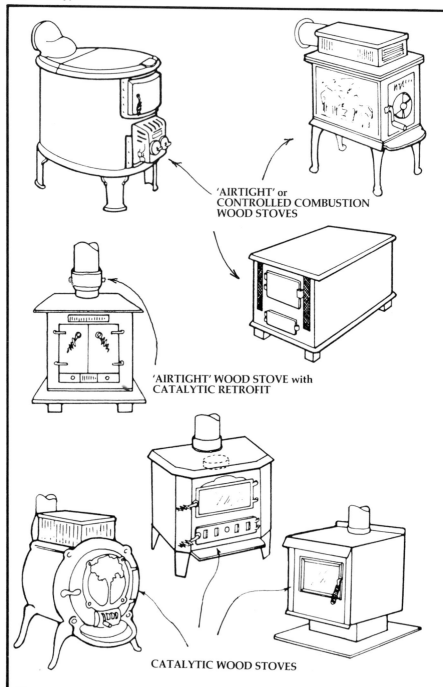

'AIRTIGHT' or
CONTROLLED COMBUSTION
WOOD STOVES

'AIRTIGHT' WOOD STOVE with
CATALYTIC RETROFIT

CATALYTIC WOOD STOVES

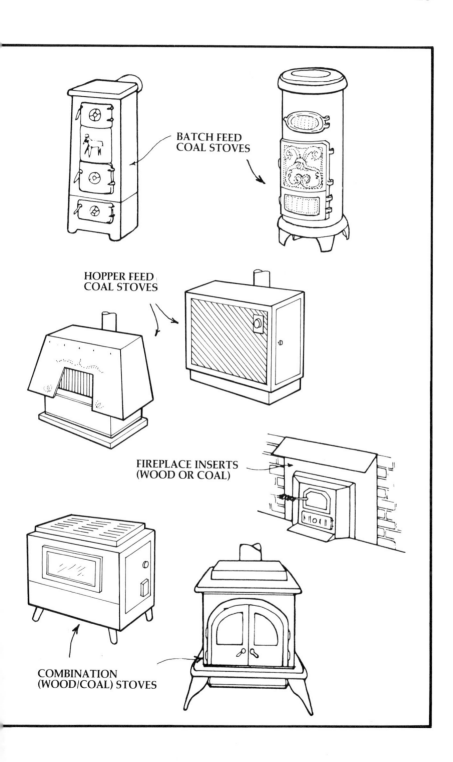

BATCH FEED
COAL STOVES

HOPPER FEED
COAL STOVES

FIREPLACE INSERTS
(WOOD OR COAL)

COMBINATION
(WOOD/COAL) STOVES

The **combination stove** can be operated as an open fireplace or a closed stove. Most of these are manufactured of cast iron and are large enough to heat one or two rooms. Some of the stoves are built with tight doors and good draft control.

Some stoves are described as dual fuel or **solid fuel** stoves. But, due to the differing combustion requirements for coal and wood, you can expect that these units will not burn either fuel as efficiently as a stove designed specifically for one fuel. On the other hand, they do provide the option to switch fuels. In some of these stoves, conversion from one fuel to the other is quite difficult and is generally done only once or twice per season. It is well to remember another option based on the adage "You can burn wood in a coal stove, but you cannot burn coal in a wood stove".

CONTROLLED COMBUSTION or 'AIRTIGHT' STOVES

Stoves are often categorized as "airtight" or "non-airtight". Since "airtight" is a misnomer (no stove is completely airtight), the solid fuel industry is gradually changing to **controlled combustion** to describe appliances which have relatively tight joints so that their rate of combustion can be controlled.

Older heaters of all types and many Franklin stoves are almost all leaky or "non-airtight." Most controlled combustion heaters have been designed and built since the early 1970's. They allow for control of the heat output by careful adjustment of the air inlet controls. Long, even burns are readily obtainable with controlled combustion heaters, but they have not always proven desirable, due to the probability of high creosote accumulation at low burning rates.

The primary air supply may not be adequate or in the correct position to supply air to support the combustion of the volatile gases, so some stoves have an additional air inlet to introduce secondary air above the flame. It is not known how effectively this secondary inlet improves operation. If too little air is admitted, incomplete combustion will result. If too much air is admitted, the gases will be cooled, affecting combustion and heat transfer.

Baffles and other stove elements which increase the length of the flame path increase the probability of complete combustion of wood volatiles.

CATALYTIC WOOD STOVES

Catalytic converters have successfully reduced automobile exhaust for several years. Now a comparable product is available for wood stoves. A precious metal catalyst makes the flammables in wood smoke burn at lower than normal temperatures. The catalyst is a thin coating of platinum or palladium applied to a honeycomb disc. (Figure 10)

Figure 10. Catalytic Wood Stoves and Add-ons

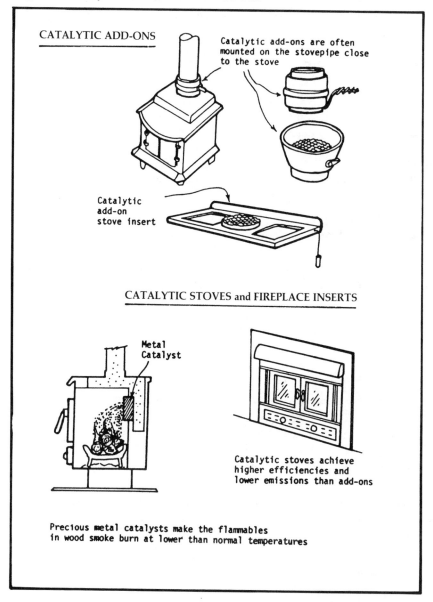

CATALYTIC ADD-ONS

Catalytic add-ons are often mounted on the stovepipe close to the stove

Catalytic add-on stove insert

CATALYTIC STOVES and FIREPLACE INSERTS

Metal Catalyst

Catalytic stoves achieve higher efficiencies and lower emissions than add-ons

Precious metal catalysts make the flammables in wood smoke burn at lower than normal temperatures

Several companies manufacture catalytic stoves, as well as add-on combusters for existing 'airtight' stoves. Catalytic systems have the potential for clean burns when the stove is filled to capacity, damped down and left for 8 to 10 hours until the next refueling.

The catalyst effectively reduces the normal temperature that the flammable gases burn from 1200°F or above, to as low as 450°F. Once the reaction begins, the temperature in the catalytic unit soars. Wood smoke is reduced, so almost no creosote or air pollution is created, and overall energy efficiencies are dramatically increased. Some testing labs have shown 25 to 30% increases in combustion efficiency in catalytic stoves over 'airtight' stoves and a more moderate increase in efficiency for add-ons.

All catalytic combustors must be replaced, usually every few years. They can be damaged when anything other than wood or newspaper is burned in the stove. Wrapping paper, painted wood, artificial logs, lighter fluids and chemical chimney cleaners are **not** to be used. A catalytic combustor adds about $200 to the cost of a new stove, and add-ons cost from $100 to $200.

PELLET-BURNING STOVES

Another type of stove designed to consume its own smoke burns pelletized wood, so air pollution is virtually eliminated. The pellet industry is rapidly growing, producing a new fuel, generally competitive in price with cord wood although the heat value is comparable to coal. Pellet stoves are expensive (over $1,000), but installation costs are less, since only a 3″ exhaust pipe is needed instead of the standard solid fuel chimney.

COAL STOVE DESIGN

Coal stove design must meet important requirements for ignition and combustion and each coal stove is designed to burn a particular type of coal. Coal requires large amounts of sustained heat for ignition and continued combustion. A **deep firebox** is necessary to encourage "back radiation" through the coals to sustain these high temperatures. (Figure 11)

Cast iron, firebrick or **fire clay** protects the metal firebox, retains heat and helps to maintain a uniform heat output. Firebrick held in place with metal brackets or cemented in place is preferred to a liner cast in the shape of the firebox, as any liner or firebrick will deteriorate eventually and require replacement.

The combustion air must be able to pass completely through the bed of burning coals. The coal is supported on a **cast iron grate** to permit even air distribution and allow for ash removal without disturbing the fire.

There are two basic types of coal stove designs, the batch feed stove and the hopper feed stove. The **batch feed** stove design is simpler and its price generally lower than the hopper feed stoves. Batch feed stoves are generally loaded from the top or side of the stove and require more care when loading to ensure that the fire is not smothered.

Figure 11. Coal Stove Requirements

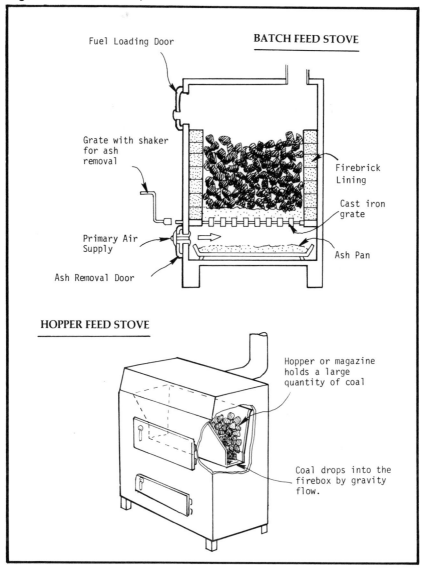

Hopper feed stoves are loaded from the top into an inner hopper which feeds the coal by gravity into the fire chamber. The burning rate is controlled more exactly since the depth of the burning coal remains relatively constant regardless of how hot the fire is burning. No burning occurs in the coal in the hopper since the top of the hopper is sealed and no heat or flue gases pass around the hopper and exit at the rear of the stove. A longer flame path for the flue gases gives higher heat transfer efficiency.

Ash removal systems which include shaker grates or slicers are necessary to remove the ashes. Coal produces 7-10 times as much ash as an equivalent amount of wood, making ash removal a daily fire-tending chore. Approximately 1 gallon of ash is produced for every 40-50 lbs of coal burned. If you choose a stove with a large well-designed **ash pan**, ash removal can be done less frequently.

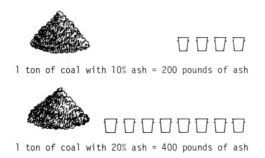

1 ton of coal with 10% ash = 200 pounds of ash

1 ton of coal with 20% ash = 400 pounds of ash

IV—Furnaces and Boilers

Most houses are designed for central heating with a furnace or boiler. Wood or coal burning furnaces are large enough to heat an entire house. Some are made to fit a furnace with hot air duct system, others a boiler and hot water system. Central heating systems keep the fuel and equipment out of your living area, but you also lose the efficiency and comfort of a radiant heat source in the most-used living area. Also, the problem of efficient heating in the milder parts of winter without overheating is compounded with the larger fireboxes of central heating systems. With the recognition of these problems, solid fuel furnaces and boilers are not as popular today as in the past.

CENTRAL HEATING OPTIONS

An **add-on furnace** or **boiler** is attached to and supplements an existing heating system. This type of unit costs less than a complete system because the existing distribution system is used. But add-on systems require additional space for the new unit, including clearance from combustible materials and space for loading and servicing. A larger or additional expansion tank may be necessary when an add-on boiler is installed.

The **multifuel furnace** or boiler can be a good choice in new homes or to replace an old heating system. These units burn wood and/or coal in combination with oil, gas, or electricity. Multifuel systems generally cost from $800-$1000 more than conventional furnaces, but they allow a choice between fuels based on expense, convenience or fuel availability. They also provide heat to automatically keep the house warm when no one is home to keep the fire burning.

Multifuel units are similar to other solid fuel burning units in operation and controls, except for the design of the firebox. Some have separate fireboxes for each fuel burned; others use only one. A firebox designed for each type of fuel is usually more efficient than a single unit. A firebox designed to burn wood efficiently is too large for burning oil, for example. Fouling of the gas or oil burner from soot, or creosote formation are some of the problems that can occur, even in the dual design.

Figure 12. Solid Fuel Central Heating

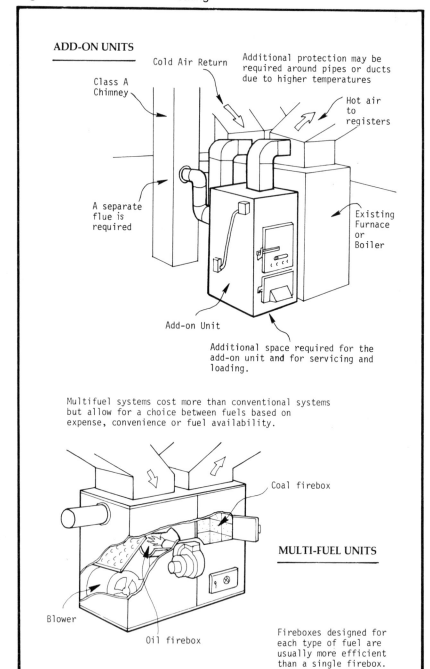

ADD-ON UNITS

Cold Air Return

Additional protection may be required around pipes or ducts due to higher temperatures

Class A Chimney

Hot air to registers

A separate flue is required

Existing Furnace or Boiler

Add-on Unit

Additional space required for the add-on unit and for servicing and loading.

Multifuel systems cost more than conventional systems but allow for a choice between fuels based on expense, convenience or fuel availability.

Coal firebox

MULTI-FUEL UNITS

Blower

Oil firebox

Fireboxes designed for each type of fuel are usually more efficient than a single firebox.

Wood chip furnaces, stoked from a hopper by a small auger are available in some areas. It is very difficult to control the feed in residential units, so they are generally restricted to commercial use. They are very efficient and the firing rate can be controlled to match the heating load. However wood chips may not be readily available and they must be stored under cover.

FEATURES

Most furnaces require less stoking than a stove, due to the large fuel capacity and controlled burning. Some of these units have a storage magazine like a hopper, which holds a large charge of wood and feeds it slowly into the combustion zone. Others have extremely large fireboxes that permit the stoking of quantities of large chunks of wood (as large as 13″ in diameter and 5′ long). Though burning large chunks is not as efficient as burning small sticks, there are savings in fuel preparation costs.

Most furnaces and boilers are thermostatically controlled. When the thermostat is not calling for heat, the primary air supply is very low and the fire continues with a very low heat output. When heat is demanded by the thermostat, the primary and secondary air supplies are opened. The fire then burns at a high rate, with near complete combustion.

In addition to stoking the fire, solid fuel furnaces require more maintenance than a gas or oil burning one. Ash removal and periodic chimney cleaning is required. The boiler or heat exchanger may need cleaning to remove deposits. Before purchasing a solid fuel furnace, talk to someone who already has one to learn more about their pros and cons.

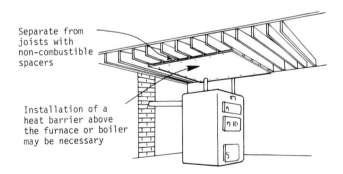

Separate from
joists with
non-combustible
spacers

Installation of a
heat barrier above
the furnace or boiler
may be necessary

Central heating systems keep the fuel
and equipment out of the living area, but
you also lose the efficiency and comfort of
a radiant heat source in the most-used
living area.

Consider the following features when selecting a furnace or boiler.

- Choose a unit approved and listed by a nationally recognized testing agency, i.e., Underwriters Laboratory, Inc., Energy Testing Laboratory of Maine, or others. Many states require that only approved units be installed. Check with the local building inspector or fire marshal before purchasing a unit.

- Steel is the most common material used for fireboxes. Some fireboxes use fire brick or cast iron liners to increase the life of the steel and to hold heat longer. A few fireboxes are made of stainless steel for longer life.

- Choose an 'airtight' unit with properly fitted seams, joints and doors. Tighter units generally achieve greater efficiencies because less heat-robbing, excess air is admitted to the firebox.

- Check whether the unit can be operated during a power failure. Most solid fuel furnaces, like conventional furnaces, depend on electricity to operate thermostats, controls, and pumps or fans to distribute heat. The units that can be operated during a power failure usually utilize the thermosiphon or gravity principle.

- Domestic hot water coils are available for many heaters and boilers. Of course, to provide hot water year around, the unit must be fired in summer as well as winter.

V—Installation

Many house fires occur because stoves are improperly installed or incorrectly connected to the chimney. Local authorities often require permits and inspections for any solid fuel stove installation, including fireplace inserts. **Before you buy and install a stove, check with your local building official.**

Home Insurance. Currently, there is no uniform national policy for insurance firms regarding stove installations. All insurance companies stress the importance of safe installations, even though they do not inspect heating systems on their own. That job is usually left to the local building inspector.

Ordinarily, there are no changes in insurance policy premiums due to the addition of a properly installed stove, although some companies impose a surcharge. However, if the appliance is improperly installed, it may be considered an unreasonable added risk, and the insurance policy can be cancelled. Because of potential conflict with an insurance company it is advisable to notify your insurance agent before you purchase or install a stove.

STOVE CLEARANCES

Many stoves are tested to Underwriters Laboratories standards by one of a number of recognized testing laboratories. Follow the installation procedure and clearances included in the operator's manual that comes with the stove.

If your stove does not have a UL listing, the National Fire Protection Association (NFPA) standards generally apply and are the basis of many local codes. Locate a stove or heater at least 36″ from unprotected woodwork, other combustible materials or furniture. Keep the stove pipe at least 18″ from an unprotected combustible ceiling. (Figure 13)

> The National Fire Protection Association (NFPA) standards for clearances from combustibles, as outlined in this chapter) can be used if your stove does not have an operator's manual outlining installation procedures.

Figure 13. Minimum Clearances from Combustibles for Unlisted Stoves

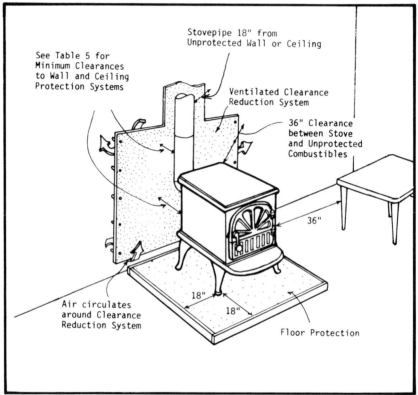

Maintaining minimum clearance is critical because wood that is continually reheated will ignite at much lower temperature than fresh wood. A new wall will start to burn at between 500-700°F. If this wall is continually heated and dried out over time, the ignition temperature can drop to 250°F. For this reason, an improper installation becomes a time bomb.

Many non-combustible or fire-resistant materials, such as plaster, cement asbestos board, gypsum board and brick are good conductors of heat. This means that the side touching the studs may be just as hot as the side exposed to the heat. Any combustible touching one of these materials can char and eventually catch fire.

FLOOR PROTECTION

Protect combustible floors from radiant stove heat, flying sparks and hot ashes by extending the material used to protect the floor. Noncombustible materials commonly used to improve the appearance of the installation, such as stone, tile, brick or marble chips can be placed over the basic NFPA recommended materials. (Table 4)

Table 4. Recommendations for Floor Protection under an Unlisted Stove

TYPE of UNIT	PROTECTIVE MATERIAL
Stove has less than 2" of open space beneath the fire chamber or base.	May not be placed on floors of combustible construction
Stove has 2" to 6" of open space beneath the fire chamber or base	Protect combustible floors with 4" hollow masonry block, laid with ends unsealed and joints matched to allow air circulation. The masonry must extend 18" on all sides of the unit and be covered with 24 gage sheet metal.
Stove has legs which provide over 6" of open space beneath the fire chamber or base.	Protect combustible floors with 2" thick closely spaced brick, concrete or stone. The masonry must extend 18" on all sides of the appliance and be covered by 24 gage sheet metal.

WALL PROTECTION

The 36″ clearance between the stove and combustibles can be reduced considerably if the walls and ceilings are protected with mineral fiber, masonry, or 24 gauge sheet metal spaced out 1″ from the combustible wall. The space allows air to circulate behind the panel to cool the wall. The spacers must be made of non-combustible material, such as a stack of washers, small diameter pipe, electrical conduit or tubing. The appearance of the approved materials may be improved with fire-resistant paint, or a facing of tile or Z-brick attached with high temperature adhesive.(Table 5, 6 and Figure 14)

Table 5. Installation Clearances from Combustible Walls and Ceilings for Unlisted Solid Fuel Heaters and Furnaces

TYPE OF PROTECTION	as WALL PROTECTION	as CEILING PROTECTION
None	36"	36"
3½" thick Masonry (brick) Wall without ventilated air space	24"	does not apply
½" thick Noncombustible Insulation Board over 1" Mineral Wool Batts, without ventilated air space	18"	24"
24 gage Sheet Metal with or without insulated backing and with ventilated air space	12"	18"
3½" thick Masonry (brick) Wall with ventilated air space	12"	does not apply
½" thick Noncombustible Insulation Board with ventilated air space	12"	18"

¹Adapted from the American National Standard ANSI/NFPA 211, Feb 1984.

Table 6. Installation Clearances from Combustible Walls and Ceilings for Stovepipes

TYPE of PROTECTION	STOVEPIPE CLEARANCE
None	18"
28 gage Sheet Metal, spaced out 1"	9"
3½" thick Masonry Wall (brick), spaced out 1" and adequately tied to the wall	9"
22 gage Sheet Metal on 1" Mineral Wool Batts, reinforced with wire and spaced out 1"	3"

NOTES:

1. Spacers and ties shall be noncombustible.

2. If a single wall connector passes through a masonry wall, maintain 1/2" open ventilated airspace between the connector and the masonry.

Figure 14. Provide Air Circulation around Heat Barriers

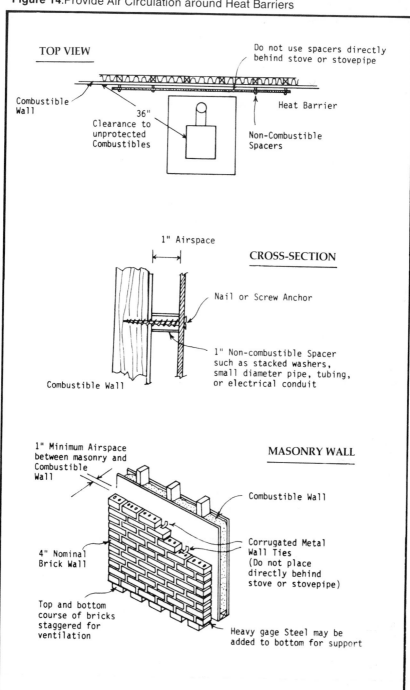

FURNACE DUCT CLEARANCES

Hot air furnace ducts require the following clearance from combustibles—18″ for the first 3′ from the furnace plenum, 6″ for the next 3′ and 1″ when more than 6′ from the plenum. (Figure 15)

Keep hot water or steam pipes 1″ from combustibles. The clearance may be reduced to 1/2″ where a pipe passes through a floor, wall or ceiling.

Figure 15. Furnace Duct Clearances

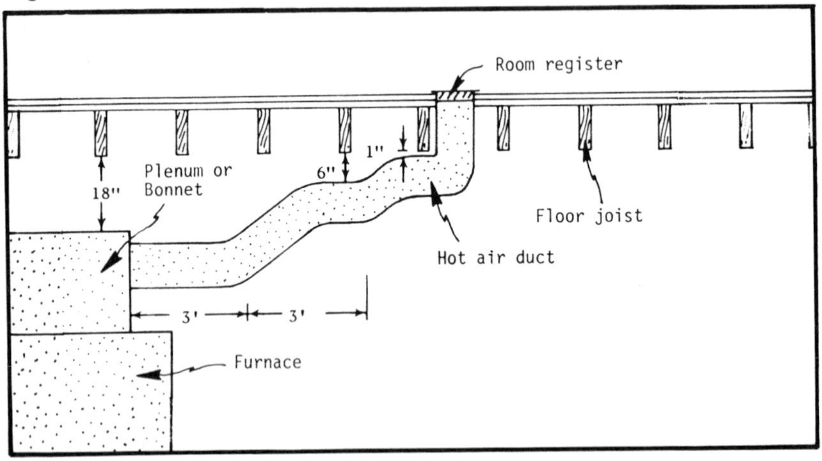

STOVEPIPE

The chimney connector or stovepipe used to connect the outlet of the firebox to the chimney is sold in various lengths. Building codes require them to be 24 gauge or thicker; lower gauge numbers indicate thicker metal. The diameter of the connector should be the same diameter as the firebox outlet. Most wood stoves use either a 6″ or 8″ connector; a smaller diameter than the firebox outlet will possibly cause improper draft.

Some stove installations require a damper either built into the stove or in the pipe near the stove to control draft and loss of volatile gases. Check the recommendation of the stove manufacturer. Add-on catalytic converters can be inserted into stovepipes to increase the efficiency of and reduce emissions from 'airtight' stoves.

Stovepipes should be short and straight and enter the chimney higher than the outlet of the stove's firebox. Keep the connector less than 10′ long to avoid excess heat loss from the flue gases and creosote accumulation.

Avoid horizontal runs. Instead, use 45° angles to create an upward slope in the connector. Try to have no more than one right angle turn between the stove and chimney.

STOVE INSTALLATION CHECKLIST

If you do not have the stove manufacturer's installation instructions, use this checklist **before** starting the first fire to ensure safe installation.

☐ 1. The stove has no broken parts or cracks that make it unsafe to operate.

☐ 2. A layer of sand or brick has been placed in the bottom of the firebox if suggested by the stove manufacturer.

☐ 3. The stove is located on a non-combustible floor or an approved floor protection material is placed under the stove.

☐ 4. Floor protection extends out 18″ on all sides.

☐ 5. The stove is spaced at least 36″ away from combustible material. If not, fire-resistant materials are used to protect woodwork and other combustible materials.

☐ 6. A chimney connector of 22 or 24 gauge metal is used.

☐ 7. The chimney connector diameter is not reduced between the stove and the chimney.

☐ 8. The total length of the chimney connector (stove pipe) is less than 10′.

☐ 9. There is at least 18″ between the top of the chimney connector and the ceiling or other combustible material.

☐ 10. The chimney connector slopes upward at least ¼ inch per foot of length toward the chimney and enters the chimney higher than the outlet of the stove firebox.

☐ 11. The connector enters the chimney horizontally through a thimble that is higher than the outlet of the stove firebox.

☐ 12. The chimney connector does not extend into the chimney flue lining.

☐ 13. The connector (stovepipe) fits snugly into the thimble. If not, a non-combustible seal is used.

☐ 14. The chimney connector does not pass through a floor, closet, concealed space or enter the chimney in the attic.

☐ 15. A UL approved ALL FUEL or HT metal chimney is used where a masonry chimney is not available or practical.

☐ 16. The chimney is in good repair.

☐ 17. The chimney flue lining is not blocked.

☐ 18. The chimney flue lining and the connector are clean.

☐ 19. A metal container with tight fitting lid is available for ash disposal.

☐ 20. The building official or fire inspector has approved the installation.

☐ 21. The company insuring the building has been notified of the installation.

☐ 22. A smoke detector is installed on or near the ceiling in an area adjacent to the stove.

☐ 23. A fire extinguisher (with at least 1A:10B:C rating) is near the entrance to the room with the stove.

VI—Chimneys

The chimney has two main purposes: to create a draft and to evacuate the gases of combustion. It also discharges some of the heat generated by the fire. The higher the chimney or the larger its cross sectional area, the greater the flow capacity. The area is more important in effecting capacity than chimney height.

The draft works on the principle that a column of heated air or gas is lighter than a column of cooler air. As the flue gases are heated, they rise in the flue and are replaced by air drawn in through the openings in the stove.

A strong draft is particularly important for coal burning to draw air through the deep, tightly packed coal bed (particularly with the smaller sizes of coal). Do not install a coal stove in a chimney with a history of backdrafting or flow reversal, since the stove will not operate well and carbon monoxide may enter the house.

FACTORS AFFECTING the DRAFT

- Increasing the height of the chimney increases the draft. For this reason, basement heating units often burn better than those located in the upper stories.

- The higher the flue gas temperature, the greater the draft. For most chimneys if the average temperature of the flue gases is kept 200°F above the outdoor temperature there should be adequate draft to burn coal. Interior chimneys or insulated chimneys (either metal or masonry) help to keep flue gas temperatures high enough to ensure good draft.

- If the chimney is too large for the size of the stove, the flue gases will be cooled. In this case a stainless steel pipe of 6-8″ diameter may be inserted the length of the chimney and 4″ beyond the top of the chimney. A fabricated cap covers the chimney top between the pipe and the flue.

- A sooty or dirty chimney will restrict the draft. Periodic cleaning is necessary.

- Well-sealed stovepipe connections and an airtight stove help achieve a strong draft.

41

If the draft is insufficient, purchasing a unit with a forced draft, usually a small blower, can solve the problem. An automatic barometric damper in the stovepipe can be used to reduce excessive draft.

CHIMNEY TYPES

Prefabricated metal chimneys are easier to erect than masonry ones. Tests at the National Bureau of Standards have shown that metal and masonry chimneys differ little with respect to draft when used under similar conditions. Metal prefabricated chimneys must be UL listed as ALL FUEL chimneys. Do not use the UL listed "Vent" as it is not insulated or ventilated enough for wood or coal burning. (Figure 16)

There are two types of metal chimneys, an insulated chimney and a triple wall chimney. Insulated prefabricated chimneys are made of a stainless steel outer casing, one inch of insulation and a stainless steel inner liner.

Triple wall chimneys are constructed either with dead air spaces between sections or such that outside air passes down between the outer walls of the triple wall chimney and up along the interior wall. This movement of air cools the chimney and may add to creosote formation.

Masonry Chimneys

The material cost for masonry block chimneys is less per foot of length than the steel prefabricated chimneys, but much more labor is required for construction. Masonry chimneys act as large heat sinks to radiate warmth into the room after the stove cools—if it is inside the house and not on an outside wall.

Existing chimneys which are unlined or in need of repair can be insulated and restored to safe functioning for solid fuel appliances. One such restoration scheme uses a lightweight, acid-resistant cement and volcanic ash compound which is inserted around an inflated rubber "flue former" sized to match your appliance capacity. Multiple flues can be created within a single large chimney and flues that bend up to 45° can also be lined.

A thimble may be permanently cemented to the chimney to facilitate removal of the connector for cleaning. Leave a small gap between the thimble and the covering material to allow either the house or chimney to settle slightly and not crack the thimble. The gap can be covered with a decorative flange. (Figure 17)

If no thimble is used, securely fasten the chimney connector to the chimney with high temperature cement. It must extend flush with the inner face of the liner. Remove combustible material within 18″ of the pipe. For a 6″ diameter pipe, this requires a $6'' + 2 \times 18'' = 42''$ diameter hole in a combustible wall. The hole may be closed in or covered with non-combustible materials such as masonry or sheet metal.

Figure 16. Prefabricated Chimneys

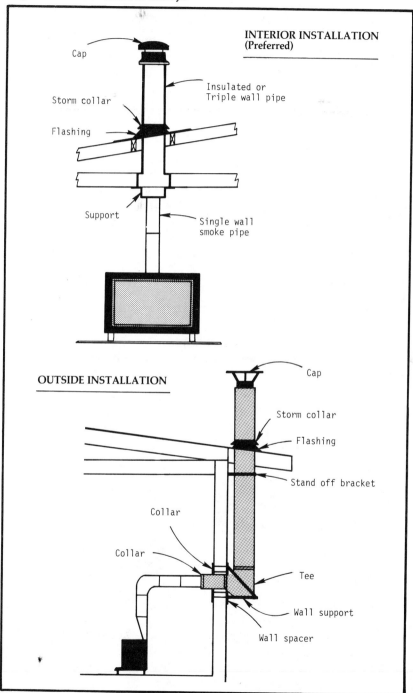

Figure 17. Chimney Connection

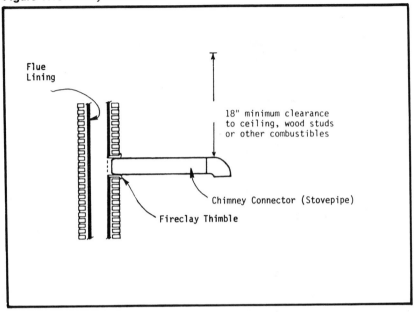

CHIMNEY REQUIREMENTS

An existing masonry fireplace should meet the following standards:

- Brick or concrete chimney walls must be at least 4″ thick and have a flue lining. Walls of stone chimneys with a flue liner must be at least 12″ thick.

- All masonry chimneys should have an intact fireclay liner at least 5/8″ thick to keep the chimney smoke-tight and prevent overheating of the chimney wall. Creosote stains on the chimney's exterior or smoke coming through the interior chimney wall suggests liner damage or cracked masonry.

- All mortar joints should be solid. If you can probe with an awl into the mortar joints more than 1/4″ have the chimney repaired.

- Unused thimbles are a problem with old masonry chimneys. It is common to find thimbles connecting the chimney flue to every room the chimney passes through. Often these thimbles are covered with metal plates and then paneling, plaster or wall paper. Not only will they conduct heat to combustible materials, but they could pop out during a chimney fire. Locate all thimbles and fill them with mortar and masonry built up to the same thickness of the chimney wall.

• Where the fireplace chimney passes through floors and ceilings, be sure the 2″ clearance between the chimney and surrounding wood structure is firestopped with a non-combustible material such as sheet metal.

Two or more Connections to One Chimney

National Fire Protection Association Standard NFPA 211 states that a connector serving a gas or oil appliance must not be connected to a flue serving a factory-built fireplace—a fireplace must have its own individual flue. Franklin stoves have an open front and should be treated as fireplaces in this respect. The standard does have an exception though. If the gas or oil appliance is listed for such an installation and is installed according to the listing, it may be connected to the flue.

NFPA Standard 211 does not allow connecting a solid fuel stove to the same flue serving appliances burning other fuels, unless it is listed for such a connection. There are three reasons for this rule. First, each time the furnace shuts off, a small amount of unburned fuel enters the chimney. A spark from the wood stove could ignite the gas and cause a small explosion. Second, the chimney is often not large enough for proper operation of the two heaters. Third, gases from one unit may come into the house through the other unit so that dangerous fumes may accumulate in the house.

CHIMNEY CAPS

A chimney cap is sometimes used to help prevent downdrafts where the chimney top is subject to wind turbulence caused by roof shape, trees, terrain, or other buildings and to keep out rain and snow. Any cap adds resistance to the system and reduces the draft. Mechanical turbines, revolving ventilators and other mechanical devices are subject to failure from creosote buildup and weather.

Often the disadvantages outweigh advantages and caps are not used. If a cap is necessary, a removable flat disk cap is simple and slows gas flow very little.

CHIMNEY HEIGHT

Extend chimneys at least 3′ above flat roofs, and at least 2′ higher than any point on a pitched roof within 10′ of the chimney. A high chimney reduces chances of down drafts caused by wind being deflected from the roof. (Figure 18)

Figure 18. Chimney Heights

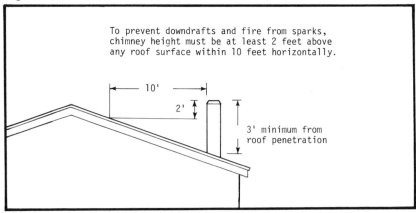

To prevent downdrafts and fire from sparks,
chimney height must be at least 2 feet above
any roof surface within 10 feet horizontally.

The flue lining of a masonry chimney should extend 4″ above the top course of brick or stone. Two inch thick cement mortar at the outside edges of the chimney top and sloped up to the flue lining directs air currents upward at the top of the flue and drains water from the top of the chimney.

CHIMNEY INSPECTION

Inspect stove pipes and chimney flues frequently for creosote build-up, especially during the first wood burning season. One method for checking stove pipes is to tap on the pipe with a metal object. The sound will change from a metal ping to a dull thud as materials build up inside the pipe. Usually creosote build-up is greatest in the horizontal sections of the stove pipe. The chimney may be inspected from the roof. If you use an 'airtight' stove, check the stove pipes frequently (weekly) until you gain experience with the stove.

CHIMNEY CLEANING

Chimney cleaning prevents chimney fires and improves the draft. How often the chimney is cleaned depends on how frequently the stove is used and how it is operated. Some need cleaning only once or twice a year; an improperly operated stove can plug up a chimney in a week. Any time an inspection shows a 1/8″ to 1/4″ thick layer of soot or creosote, the chimney requires cleaning.

One of the advantages of coal over wood is the absence of a creosote problem. However, burning coal does deposit fly ash and particles of solid carbon in the stovepipe and flue. This soot reduces the heat value of the fuel by interfering with the draft, and can hold sulfuric and hydrochloric acids along the flue pipe and chimney. This corrosive mixture can cause rapid deterioration of steel chimneys and slower deterioration in masonry chimneys. While not as readily flammable as creosote, soot can ignite and fuel a chimney fire, which could damage the chimney or spread to other parts of the house.

Chimneys are normally cleaned by mechanical means to scrape off any loose creosote build-up. **Stiff chimney cleaning brushes** constructed to match the size of the chimney flue are pushed through the chimney with extension rods or pipe or pulled with ropes on either end of the brush. In some cases a weight attached to the bottom of the brush will drag the brush to the bottom of the chimney where it is then pulled up with a rope. (Figure 19)

Figure 19. Chimney Cleaning

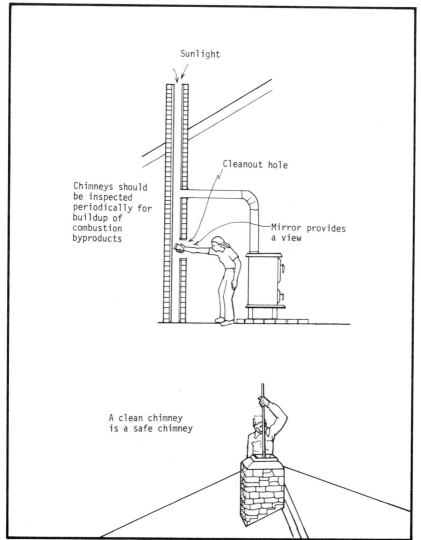

If you clean the chimney, be very careful when climbing on high, steep roofs. You may instead want to hire a chimney sweep who has the proper safety equipment and is knowledgeable in chimney inspection. Many professionals carry large vacuum cleaners to clean up the soot.

Fireplace flues present additional cleaning problems. Where possible, remove the fireplace damper so scrapings do not lodge behind it during the cleaning. Then cover the fireplace opening by taping a plastic cover over it. **Be sure to clean or vacuum the smoke shelf above the fireplace where scrapings accumulate.**

Chemicals, such as sodium chloride or table salt, are sometimes used as a chimney cleaner. The chemical combines with water released from a hot fire to form a weak acid that dissolves small amounts of creosote. They may corrode metal chimneys and stove parts. Some of the newer chemical products have proven more effective in chimney cleaning and even in removing glazed creosote. Some of these products are available only to licensed chimney sweeps. They must not be used in catalytic wood stoves as they will damage the catalytic converter.

Do not rely on chemical chimney cleaners alone. If chemicals are used, check that they are non-corrosive and continue frequent inspection.

HEATING SYSTEM MAINTENANCE

A build-up of soot and ash on the surfaces of the stove or furnace and stovepipe acts as an insulator, inhibiting the transfer of heat to the house. Use a wire brush to clean the heater interior and flue when soot builds up to a 1/4″ thickness.

For rust protection during the summer, remove all fuel and ashes, clean the interior of the stove or the heat transfer surfaces of a furnace or boiler and coat with a light oil or silicone spray. An open coffee can of silia gel inside the heater will absorb moisture.

Stokers require occasional lubrication of the bearings and gear motor, cleaning of the fan, and oiling of the stoker surfaces to prevent corrosion. Remove coal from the hopper and augers during the summer. Clean and oil as described above.

Draft leaks affect both the operation and safety of the installation. Seal any cracks between stovepipe connections and castings with furnace cement.

CHIMNEY FIRES

Even with the most conscientious cleaning habits, stove owners still face some danger of fire. A properly installed stove and chimney can withstand an **occasional** chimney fire. However, the ignition temperature of new house framing is about 500°F. Over a period of years, as this wood is repeatedly heated by fires, the wood will ignite at a lower temperature. Thus, everything possible should be done to reduce the frequency of such fires.

Prepare for a fire with an emergency plan for family members. Designate exits and an outside meeting place; discuss special problems you anticipate. Have on hand, and know how to use, several multi-purpose (ABC) dry chemical extinguishers. Locate them between the stove and exit and between the stove and your bed. Install a smoke detector in the vicinity of bedroom areas and near the basement stairs. Be alert to a roaring noise and sparks from the chimney. (Figure 20)

Figure 20. Fire Extinguishers and Smoke Detectors should be part of every stove installation

When you realize a chimney fire has started, arouse everyone in the house and start your emergency plan. If the fire has spread to the house, get everyone out and stay out. Call the fire department from a neighbor's.

If the fire is restricted within the chimney, close stove openings, draft controls and dampers to cut the air supply to the fire. Then call the fire department.

As part of your emergency planning, decide how you would fight a chimney fire. The best attack point would be through the cleanout door of the chimney. Do not attempt to use the cleanout of a metal "T" connection on a metal chimney; this is too close to the fire.

The cleanout door of a masonry chimney may have an active fire behind it, so be careful when opening it to discharge the dry chemical extinguisher. Observe the precautions outlined below for fighting a fire through the stove.

If a cleanout door is not available, or is not feasible to use for fighting the fire, then you have to fight the fire through the stove. Expect that intensive, violent burning is occurring. Stovepipes may be red hot! A chimney fire can have temperatures in excess of 2000°F. Do not look directly into the fire, and keep the stove door between you and the fire.

First open the damper, then **cautiously** open the door. Be careful of flames that may flashback toward you. Step back from the stove, and use a fire extinguishing chimney flare, available at most stove dealers, or a dry chemical fire extinguisher. Hold extinguisher upright, and spray in short bursts until the extinguisher is empty. To avoid breathing fumes from these chemicals, hold your breath for several seconds. Leave the door open for a few seconds to allow the chemicals to be drawn up the chimney, then close everything again.

If the fire does not seem to slow down and the fire department has not arrived, try another extinguishing treatment. Be alert for flash backs when reopening the stove door.

The use of water on a hot chimney or stove can crack the stove and damage the chimney. Make dry chemical extinguishers part of your original stove installation!

After the chimney fire is out, inspect the chimney from base to top for damage and make any needed repairs. If a metal chimney is involved check for damage. Discoloration or bulges in metal and gaps at the joints can indicate a potential source of future trouble.

Many chimney fires start because the fire in the stove gets out of hand. This can happen if you use your stove as a trash burner or let the flames from a large mass of paper go up the chimney. Many chimney fires result from heavy loading of a stove and then reducing the air supply for a long burn. The wood dries out, the volatiles evaporate, and a full load of material remains to burn fast and furious.

VII— Wood as a Fuel

BUYING FIREWOOD

Measurement Units

When purchasing firewood one is often faced with a confusing array of measurement units. Firewood is normally sold by the cord or by a fraction of a cord (a requirement in many states). A standard cord is a compact stack 8' long, 4' high, and 4' wide. Be sure you have a clear understanding with the seller, preferably in writing, of the amount of wood being sold. (Figure 21)

Figure 21. Wood Measurement Units

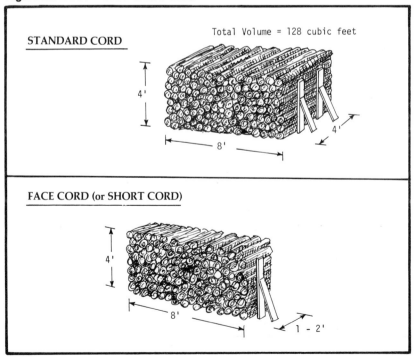

STANDARD CORD

Total Volume = 128 cubic feet

4'

8'

4'

FACE CORD (or SHORT CORD)

4'

8'

1 - 2'

The measurement units include the air space between the sticks. Thus the amount of solid wood depends upon whether the sticks are straight or crooked, round or split, and large or small in diameter. The variation is considerable as a standard cord may contain from 60 to 110 cubic feet of solid wood. A commonly used conversion from gross volume to solid wood content of hardwood sticks 3"-8" in diameter is 80 cubic feet per standard cord. Larger diameters of round wood or split wood, neatly stacked, usually yield more solid wood per cord.

Other factors to consider when buying wood are:

- A standard cord cut into shorter lengths will always stack in less space than originally because many of the crooks are eliminated and some wood is lost as sawdust.

- A standard cord contains about two to four times as much wood as a face cord, depending on stick length.

- A cord of green wood will shrink at least 8% in volume during seasoning.

Firewood is sometimes sold by the load or by weight. Of course, the amount of wood in a "truck load" varies greatly depending upon the type of vehicle. A pick-up truck with a bed 4' wide, 19" deep and 8' long will hold one 16" face cord. A dump truck may hold up to 4 standard cords. Large pulpwood trucks with a wood rack will hold from 6 to 9 standard cords.

When buying wood by weight, try not to buy water; that is, **look for the driest wood possible**. In general, when dried to about 20% moisture content (oven dry basis), dense hardwoods (oak, hickory and maple) weigh about 4,000 pounds per standard cord while softwoods weigh half that amount. A cord of green wood weighs up to a ton more than dry wood depending on the species.

The price fuelwood dealers charge varies depending upon the amount of wood, species, seasoning, whether it is delivered or not and the geographic location. Sometimes one can buy economically by ordering well in advance and in large quantities. Industrial wood scraps (slabs, trim and edging) can often be purchased directly from a sawmill or other wood-using business. These sticks are usually small enough for small fireplaces and stoves or they may be split for kindling.

HEATING VALUE

The heat derived from the combustion of wood depends upon the density or concentration of woody material, resin, ash, and water in the wood. The first three features vary depending on the tree species and its growth rate, while the latter depends on the species, the season in which the tree was cut and the seasoning procedures used. In general, the heaviest or most dense woods, when seasoned, have the greatest heating value. Lighter woods give about the same heat value per pound as heavier hardwoods, but, because they are less dense, they give less heat per cord or cubic foot. The heating values per air-dried standard cord of numerous woods compared to other fuels are given in Table 7.

Table 7. Heat Value of Various Woods Compared to other Fuels

A CORD OF AIR-DRY WOOD EQUALS	Tons of Coal	Gallons of Fuel Oil	Therms of Natural Gas	Kilowatt Hours of Electricity
Hickory, Hop hornbeam (ironwood), Black locust, White Oak, Apple	0.9	127	174	3800
Beech, Sugar maple, Red oak, Yellow birch, White ash	0.8	115	160	3500
Gray and paper birch, Black walnut, Black cherry, Red maple, Tamarack(Larch), Pitch pine	0.7	99	136	3000
American elm, Black and green ash, Sweet gum, Silver and bigleaf maple, Red cedar, Red pine	0.6	90	123	2700
Poplar, Cottonwood, Black willow, Aspen, Butternut, Hemlock, Spruce	0.5	75	102	2200
Basswood, White pine, Balsom fir, White cedar	0.4	63	87	1900

ASSUMPTIONS-

Wood: 1 cord = 128 cubic feet of wood and air or 80 cubic feet of solid wood at 20% moisture content. Net or low heating value of one pound of dry wood is 6,200 Btu. Efficiency of the burning unit is 50%.

Coal: Heating value is 12,500 Btu per pound. Efficiency of the burning unit is 50%.

Fuel Oil: Heating value is 138,000 Btu per gallon burned at an efficiency of 75%.

Natural gas: One therm = 100,000 Btu = 100 cubic feet. Efficiency of burning is 75%.

Electricity: One KWh = 3,412 Btu. Efficiency is 100%.

CUTTING YOUR OWN WOOD

The romantic notion of "firewood-gathering" should actually be thought of as timber harvesting. It may indeed be healthy exercise, but it is also one of the most dangerous professions in the United States. Proper education on safe chainsaw operation and proper tree felling techniques cannot be learned entirely from a book or a film; only many hours of supervised practice will suffice. Appendix A: Cutting Firewood with a Chainsaw will introduce you to some of the basics of safe chainsaw operation.

For those owning a woodlot, cutting trees for firewood can improve the quality and rate of growth of the remaining trees, and it is the least expensive means of obtaining firewood. But cutting trees is dangerous work that takes personal time and a vehicle for hauling. It generally takes about 4 to 10 hours of work to ready a standard cord of wood for the fire. The beginner may take longer.

A typical woodlot has a sustaining yield of about ½ cord per acre per year. A tree with a 12″ to 14″ base will generally yield ½ a standard cord; ¼ cord from the trunk and ¼ cord from the branches. A 20 acre wood lot can easily provide a continuous supply of firewood for most households.

To obtain the most economic value, cut those trees that will give more room for the growth of the best remaining trees in the woodlot. Formerly, an owner frequently cut the straight, well-pruned trees for firewood, because they split easier than their crooked, limby neighbors. Such cutting rapidly reduces the timber value of the woodlot. Crooked trees with many branches are often the trees which environmentally should be removed for firewood, although they require more time and energy per volume of wood produced. Utilize diseased, dead, and otherwise damaged trees, unless they are necessary for wildlife protection. Sometimes, of course, straight trees are removed to reduce crowding of equally good or better trees. Try to space future timber trees an average of 20 feet apart.

The art of "culling" a woodlot requires good judgment. Woodlot owners unfamiliar with woodlot improvement techniques may obtain technical advice and service through the State Conservation Department, the State Forester, Extension Forester or a consulting forester.

If you do not own a woodlot it is sometimes possible to buy cutting and salvage rights on municipal, state, federal, or privately owned lands for nominal cost. Some of these cuttings involve selected thinning of public woodlots while others are salvage operations in logged areas. Utility company right-of-ways, land clearing operations and areas that have recently been logged are other sources to be considered. However, areas accessible to the typical homeowner are rapidly becoming scarce. Generally, the distance that a person is willing to hand-carry wood to a road is dictating the extent of public thinning operations. Some state agencies and private companies will soon be out of the firewood business unless accessibility is improved or professionally removed tree-length logs are made available at roadside.

Be resourceful. Look for as many sources as possible for your fuel supplies. But start early, the fall is not the best time to work up a firewood supply for the forthcoming winter. Try to cut your wood a year ahead.

Figure 22. Improve the value of your woodlot while gathering fuelwood.

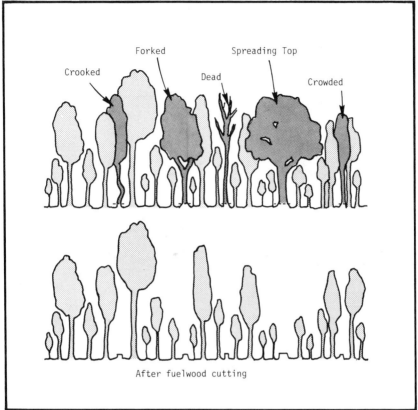

CHARACTERISITICS OF WOOD
========================

When considering the type of wood to burn, other characteristics in addition to heat value are often important. These characteristics include ease of splitting, ease of ignition and burning, extent of smoking, extent of sparking, and coaling qualities, or the ability to form long-lived coals. Table 8 lists characteristics of commonly used fuelwoods. Moisture content of the wood and the number of knots also affect these characteristics.

If you cut your own firewood or split kindling and logs, the splitting characteristics of wood are very important. Short lengths of straight-grained, knot-free wood will split easily. Green wood and softwoods usually, but not always, split more easily than dry wood and hardwoods. Sometimes, frozen wood splits easily. Straight-grained cottonwood, aspen, fir and pine split easily and are best for kindling. In contrast, woods with interlocking grain, like American elm and sycamore may be very difficult to split.

Table 8. Characteristics of Commonly Burned Woods

SPECIES	SPLIT-ABILITY	EASE of STARTING	HEAVY SMOKE	SPARKS	COALING QUALITIES
Apple	Hard	Hard	No	Few	Excellent
Ash	Medium	Fair	No	Few	Good
Beech	Hard	Hard	No	Few	Excellent
Birch	Medium	Easy	No	Moderate	Good
Cedar	Easy	Easy	Yes	Many	Poor
Cherry	Medium	Hard	No	Few	Excellent
Cottonwood	Easy	Easy	Medium	Moderate	Good
Elm	Hard	Fair	Medium	Few	Good
Hemlock	Hard	Easy	Medium	Many	Poor
Hickory	Medium	Fair	No	Moderate	Excellent
Locust,Black	Hard	Hard	No	Few	Excellent
Maple	Medium	Hard	No	Few	Excellent
Oak	Hard	Hard	No	Few	Excellent
Pine	Easy	Easy	Medium	Moderate	Fair-Poor
Poplar,Yellow	Easy	Easy	Medium	Moderate	Fair
Spruce, Norway	Medium	Easy	Yes	Many	Poor
Sycamore	Medium	Fair	Medium	Few	Good
Tamarack(Larch)	Easy	Easy	Medium	Moderate	Good
Walnut	Medium	Easy	No	Few	Good
Willow	Medium	Easy	No	Moderate	Poor

Softwoods, being resinous, are easy to ignite and burn rapidly with a high, hot flame. However, they burn out quickly and require frequent attention. Some resinous softwoods, such as cedar, juniper, larch, hemlock and spruce contain moisture pockets which can be troublesome. Upon heating, trapped gases and water vapor build up pressure in these pockets resulting in "pops" which throw sparks. Such sparking can be a potential fire hazard especially in fireplaces without proper screens. Sparking is another reason to reduce the moisture content of wood as much as possible before burning.

Hardwoods are generally more difficult to ignite, burn less vigorously and with a shorter flame, but last longer and produce more coals than softwoods. White birch typically is easy to ignite due to its papery, resinous bark. Oak gives the most uniform and shortest flame and produces steady, glowing coals.

Artificial logs (composite of sawdust, chips, wax, chemicals and starch binder) are used in fireplaces for their convenience and ease of starting. Most of these logs should not be burned in a stove as their combustion characteristics and gaseous outputs are considerably different from wood logs. Be sure to read and follow manufacturer's instructions.

SEASONING WOOD

Eliminating moisture from firewood before storing it indoors or burning it greatly reduces potential insect pest nuisances, firewood ignition problems and creosote build-up in the chimney. Any moisture in the wood reduces the recoverable heat because water absorbs heat in the process of being changed to steam. When air dried under cover, most types of wood will reach approximately 20% moisture content.

The moisture in the wood of living trees varies among species, within a species, and even within a single tree. Frequently, there is a significant difference between the quantity of moisture contained in the central column of heartwood of a tree and the outer layers of sapwood which is surrounded with bark. For example, freshly cut American beech has been found to have a heartwood moisture content of 72%. In contrast, heartwood moisture contents in American elm, northern red oak, and white ash are 95, 80 and 46% respectively.

The greater the surface area without bark that is exposed to air, the more rapid the drying. Short sticks dry more rapidly because moisture moves most freely along the grain. Wood greater than 8″in diameter or longer than 4′ dries very slowly. Reduce the size of such sticks by splitting and/or sawing and stack in loose piles raised off the ground to increase air circulation.

The greater the surface area without bark that is exposed to air, the more rapid the drying

Seasoning can be accelerated greatly by stacking fuelwood in a sunny location and covering it with clear plastic sheeting. In sunny weather, temperatures under the cover will rise much higher than outside, warming the wood and evaporating the contained moisture. The water vapor produced either escapes or condenses on the plastic covering; therefore some air movement is necessary or the plastic sheet must be turned periodically, to remove condensation. It is also desirable to hold the plastic away from the rough ends of the wood to prevent abrasion, allow air to flow, and keep any condensate from re-wetting the wood. (Figure 23)

Figure 23. Solar Wood Dryer

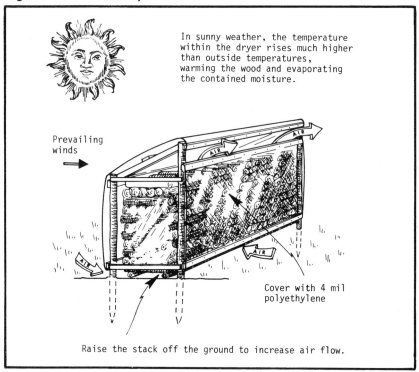

In sunny weather, the temperature within the dryer rises much higher than outside temperatures, warming the wood and evaporating the contained moisture.

Prevailing winds

Cover with 4 mil polyethylene

Raise the stack off the ground to increase air flow.

Many plastic cover arrangements are possible. Thin 2 mil, clear polyethylene sheeting sold for drop cloths or garden mulching tears easily. The 4 mil thickness is more satisfactory and less costly than 6 mil. Any clear polyethylene deteriorates badly after a few months of exposure to full sunlight, so the stack may have to be re-roofed to remain dry over winter.

A small scale can be used to check if firewood is still seasoning. Weigh a basket or bag of a few pieces of firewood. Mark them and place them back in the wood pile. Then weigh them again in about a month. If they have lost weight, the wood is still drying. Cracks that appear in the end of logs are good signs that the wood is seasoning.

Generally, wood that is cut to length, split, and stacked in the open, preferably with a cover, during the winter should be seasoned by the next heating season.

STORING WOOD

Firewood is best stored outdoors, under cover and near the house so that valuable space in the house is not used, insects are kept outside, and the dirt problem is reduced. It can be stored in a wood shed, utility building, garage or under a sheet of plastic or sheet metal roofing. Be sure to keep an air space between the wood and any covering.

If sufficient space is available under a roof, seasoning and storage can be accomplished in one handling. This practice eliminates the extra handling of moving wood dried outside into a covered storage area.

Outside, wood will dry to between 14% and 25% moisture content depending on humidity, temperature, and wind. In a garage or woodshed it may dry to about 18% moisture content; and wood may dry to about 12% in the house.

End braces can be used if you have difficulty stacking wood and if the pile collapses at either end. Constructed with two-by-fours, end braces are like book ends and can be built to accurately measure a standard cord. The planks, 2 x 4's, etc. beneath the woodpile keep the bottom row above wet ground.

In some homes, a wood box can be constructed inside the house, convenient to the wood stove and which has loading access outside.

Operating Techniques

Review the section on combustion basics in Chapter 1. The combustion rate is controlled by the amount of air that is supplied to the fire. With more air, the rate of burn increases and more heat is generated. The rate of burn is also governed by the size of the fuel. Small kindling wood burns rapidly to start a fire and large pieces burn slowly to sustain a fire overnight.

If only the exact amount of air needed for combustion were fed to the fire, maximum efficiency would not be reached. In reality the air and combustibles can not be perfectly mixed, so some unburned particles escape without coming into contact with the oxygen. Some excess of air, usually 20 to 50 percent, is needed to get more complete burning. On the other hand, excess air cools the fire and takes more heat up the chimney.

CREOSOTE

Smoke forms because the combustion process of wood is never absolutely complete. The smoke contains the chemicals which form a dark brown or black substance called creosote, a complex mixture of compounds.

Flue gases leaving the fire cool as heat is absorbed by the stovepipe-chimney system. If the flue gas temperature drops below about 270°F, these unburned volatiles and water vapor condense. In time, the water evaporates leaving dark, highly combustible creosote on the stovepipe and chimney walls.

The amount of creosote condensing on the surfaces of the system varies according to the density of the smoke, the temperature of the chimney's surface and the type and moisture content of wood being burned. Dense smoke from a smoldering fire is most likely to form large amounts of creosote. (Figure 24)

Combustion of accumulated creosote in the chimney and stovepipe is likely to occur during a very hot fire. A very intense fire results, creating a roaring noise and producing flames and sparks from the top of the chimney. Chimney fires may crack the chimney tile, loosen mortar, and burn the roof; they are [not] a safe way to remove creosote from a system.

A low or smoldering fire tends to build up creosote. When there is no flame or only a very small flame to ignite the volatiles, these unburned combustibles go up the chimney. When a fire is first started, the chimney surfaces are relatively cool, so creosote accumulates rapidly. When only burning coals remain, little creosote is formed. If you are buying your first wood burning stove, choose the smaller rather than the larger model. A small stove with an actively burning fire will produce less creosote than a large stove damped down to restrict rapid burning. Even though a smaller stove requires more frequent loading, the wood burns more efficiently because the fire is hotter.

Figure 24.Creosote Formation

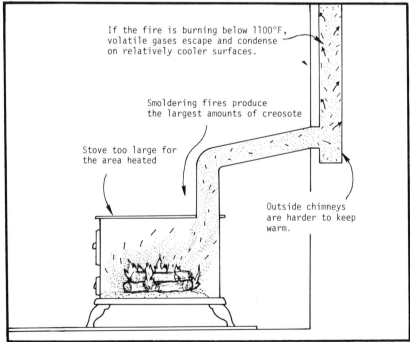

Stove design as well as operation affects creosote formation. Stoves which have a long flame path in the stove are working to keep the volatiles in the stove and at a high enough ignition temperature to ignite before leaving the stove. The catalytic stoves and add-ons discussed in Chapter 3 are designed to burn volatile gases at lower temperatures and to eliminate most of the creosote problems.

Reduce creosote formation in 'airtight' stoves by the following procedures:

- Open the air inlet to establish a hot fire quickly; then close it to the desired position. Remember that heat is absorbed by the new fuel to heat the wood and drive off water and combustible volatiles. Leave air inlets open until the new charge of wood is burning well; then restrict inlets to allow continued **active burning** instead of a roaring fire.

- A stovepipe thermometer is a useful and inexpensive devise to help you monitor combusion temperatures and reduce creosote formation.

- Do not try to increase the time between refueling by restricting the wood's air supply and/or by filling the firebox as full as possible. Add a partial load (about 1/3 capacity) when refueling. Loading more than one-third of capacity cools the stove, so combustion gases driven from the wood are not ignited and are lost up the chimney. Lengthening the time between refuelings tends to increase creosote buildup.

- Learn how to burn all types of wood. Air dried hardwood burns best. However, when you must use green, wet, or softwood, try to get the same heat output from the stove as with air-dried hardwood.

- **Starting with a clean chimney**, open all air inlets in an airtight stove for 15 to 30 minutes every day. The resulting hot fire will safely remove the small amounts of creosote formed in the chimney. **DO NOT** get the pipe or stove red hot. Follow this practice every day after the chimney is clean; an infrequent hot fire can start a serious chimney fire.

The preceding steps encourage you to maintain a hot fire and chimney so that combustion is nearly complete and creosote formation is reduced to a minimum. These practices will sometimes overheat the room, particularly in late spring and early fall. To maintain a comfortable room temperature and make the wood last longer, wood stoves are often operated at reduced draft; so they produce creosote in greater amounts. For better results with moderate outdoor temperatures, burn small pieces of wood to produce a quick, hot fire. Then let it burn out instead of maintaining a slow, smoldering fire.

STOVE OPERATION

Before starting the fire, open the stovepipe damper and baffle bypass damper, if present, to allow for removal of the large amount of smoke generated when a fire is started.

If the unit has been used, check to see that there are at least 2″ of clearance between the grate and the ash pan or ash pit for the air supply. Reduce the ash level on top of the grate to about 1″. The thin ash layer insulates the bottom of the fire and reflects the heat upward. Also, any small pieces of charcoal left from the previous fire will provide heat for the new fire.

To start the fire, crumple several pieces of newspaper and form a 2″ or 3″ layer over the bottom of the firebox. Avoid slick magazine pages as they do not burn well.

Add a layer of kindling, crisscrossing the pieces so that air and heat can get through. The best kindling is dry softwood such as pine, spruce, or hemlock. Dead twigs, scrap lumber, and small pieces of pressed logs also work well. The drier they are, the better. Try to keep a good supply under cover at all times. Kindling must be less than one inch in cross-section to ignite and burn rapidly. Split sticks work better than round because they have a greater surface area. Before lighting, add three or four larger split pieces on top. Light the paper and close the door to establish the draft and keep heat within the fire box.

Refueling

When the kindling is burning and after a bed of coals forms, add a few more pieces of dry wood. Again, smaller pieces of split wood will catch more quickly. Leave about an inch between pieces to establish paths and to reflect heat from one piece to the other to keep up the temperature. A single large piece of wood does not burn well because the heat spreads through the piece and radiates away to the metal surfaces of the stove. The wood surface temperature does not stay high enough, so the fire does not grow.

If your fire fails, move the logs to one side of the fire box, add more paper and kindling, and relight. The logs should ignite this time as some drying and charring has occurred and they are already warm. Do not pour on any flammable liquid as the glowing embers could cause an explosive fire.

After the fire is burning brightly and you feel some heat from the front, add another layer of wood. Until the stove is fully warmed use split pieces up to four or five inches across. Save large pieces for cold weather when the stove will be run at full capacity or when you want to carry a fire overnight. Large chunks burn well when they are placed to one side of the fire box and smaller pieces are fed next to it. The smaller pieces dry out the chunk and eventually turn it to charcoal which burns with even heat for an extended period.

On manual draft systems, keep an eye on the fire so you can reduce the draft once the unit gets up to temperature. Automatic control systems adjust themselves as the thermostat is satisfied.

If you have been operating a controlled combustion or 'airtight' stove at reduced draft for some time, do not immediately open the door. Open the air inlets and wait 20 to 30 seconds before opening the door. Wood burning with a low air supply could cause flames to shoot out through the opening toward the oxygen source. Stand to the side of the door and keep the door between you and the firebox, if possible.

SMOKY FIRES

Watch the smoke leaving the chimney, when you are burning wood. In a properly operated stove, most of what you see is water vapor which dissipates within a few feet from the chimney. If the smoke lingers on or trails across to the neighbors, your fire is not burning completely.

Six main causes and cures of Smoky fires are:

- **Wet wood.** Green or wet firewood causes smoke problems as much of the heat of the fire is used to dry the wood. The cure is to keep a hot fire going and to use seasoned dry wood. If green or wet wood must be burned, split it finer and mix it with dry wood. Softwoods may cause smoky fires because of the resin in the wood.

- **Flue too large.** Many older houses have a large central chimney with several fireplaces and flue openings. If this chimney is used with only one stove or heater there may not be adequate draft to keep the column of smoke rising. By reducing the cross sectional area of the top of the chimney or installing a stove pipe through the center of the flue, the smoke problem should be solved.

- **Obstructed flue.** Often stove pipes or flues become partially filled with soot and creosote. Cure this problem by checking flues and stove pipes once a month during the heating season and cleaning them when a buildup starts to occur.

- **Downdrafts.** Nearby trees, buildings or roof projections often cause downdrafts during windy periods. Raising the height of the chimney, removing the obstruction or placing a cap on the chimney may correct the problem.

- **Lack of oxygen.** A fire needs oxygen to burn properly. In the past, most installations relied on air infiltration from the

outside through cracks around doors, windows and vents. In
a tight, well-insulated house, infiltration has been reduced to
a minimum. This problem can be compounded if there are
several large appliances requiring venting, such as an oil or
gas furnace, water heater, etc. This lack of air can sometimes
cause smoke to be pulled back into the house through an
adjacent flue. Opening the basement door or a nearby
window an inch or installing a 4″ air intake below the stove
will generally eliminate this problem. Screen the outside of
an air inlet and provide a damper on the inside.

- **Exhaust vents** in other areas of a weatherized house can be
a major cause of weak drafts and/or smoky fires.

ASH REMOVAL and DISPOSAL

Too many ashes in the firebox restrict air flow and reduce the burning area. A
layer, 1″-2″ deep, is desirable to support the fire and insulate the bottom of the
fire box. Excess ash is removed, usually once or twice a week.

The disposal of wood ash is not a major problem since the volume of ash is
small—about a bushel of ashes per standard cord of firewood. Ash residue is
beneficial as a fertilizer applied at a rate of 10 pounds per 100 square feet per
year.

Many house fires have started when ashes thought to be cold were placed in a
paper or plastic container. Hot embers ignited the container and the house or
garage where they were stored. **Store ashes in a non-combustible container.**

VII— Coal as a Fuel

Coal is the result of the slow decomposition of vegetable matter, subjected for a long period to heat and pressure underneath the surface of the earth. The changes which take place in the formation of coal result in the production of various intermediate products, as follows: Cellulose $\longrightarrow$ Peat $\longrightarrow$ Lignite $\longrightarrow$ Various Coals. The process through which the cellulose has passed in the formation of coal is known as carbonization.

The combustible portions of coal are fixed carbons, volatile matter (gaseous compounds of hydrogen and carbon) and small amounts of sulfur. In combination with these are noncombustible elements—moisture and mineral impurities that form ash. The various ranks and grades of coal differ in the proportions of these elements and in the heat content. (Figure 25)

TYPES OF COAL

Anthracite (hard coal), the preferred coal for home heating, is hard, compact and shiny black. It produces little or no smoke in burning and does not soften and fuse together, so firing and ash removal can be automated. Although it is difficult to ignite, it is longer burning than other coals. Most anthracite coal comes from a relatively small region in Pennsylvania, so shipping costs limit its use generally to the Northeast.

The coal industry has standardized sizes of anthracite (Table 9). Heating units are designed to burn a specific type and size of coal, the most typical sizes being chestnut ('nut') or pea for stoves and stove coal for furnaces and boilers.

Bituminous coal (soft coal) is not as desirable as hard coal since it creates dust when burned at a low rate and may contain a high percentage of sulfur. It is found in more areas of the country than anthracite and is, therefore, less expensive in most regions because of lower transportations costs. It is used domestically in areas where it is mined, but its primary use is in electric generation and in industry. Many states have rigid regulations regarding its use.

Cannel coal (fireplace coal) is a type of bituminous coal which ignites easily and burns with a luminous, smoky flame. It can be burned in fireplaces, but must not be burned in a stove, since it tends to overheat the stove.

Figure 25. Comparison of Composition and Heat Value of Various Sample Coals

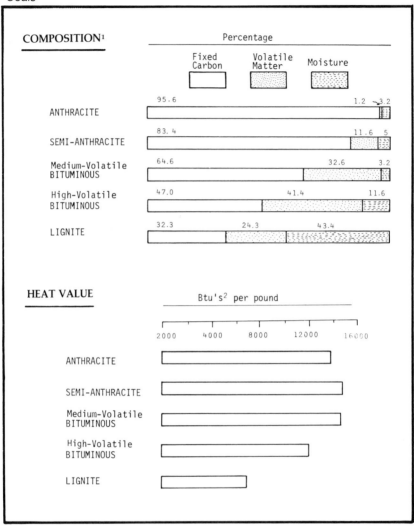

[1]The fixed carbon and volatile matter are calculated on an ash-free basis, because ash in coal varies without regard to rank.

[2]Btu or British Thermal Unit is the amount of energy required to raise the temperature of one pound of water 1° F.

Table 9. Standardized Sizes of Anthracite

NAME	SIZE	TYPICAL HEATER
Egg	2 7/16 - 3"	Large furnaces & boilers
Stove	1 5/8 - 2 7/16"	Furnaces & boilers
Chestnut "Nut"	13/16 - 1 5/8"	Stoves
Pea	9/16 - 13/16"	Stoves with hoppers and other stoves in mild weather.
Buckwheat, No. 1	5/16 - 9/16"	Stoves with hoppers & mechanical stokers

¹Smaller sizes—Rice (No.2 Buckwheat), Barley (No.3 Buckwheat) and No. 4 Buckwheat are rarely used in domestic heating.

Coke is a high grade bituminous coal, from which the moisture and most of the volatiles have been removed. It has a high heat value, burns clean, and is most successfully burned in stoves and furnaces with large fireboxes. It is not readily available.

Lignite (brown coal) is a fuel between true coal and peat. When it is mined it contains a large percentage of water, sometimes as much as 50%. When dry, its heat value compares favorably with soft coal. It occurs in immense deposits in North Dakota and Texas.

PURCHASING COAL

Buy the exact type and size of coal suitable for your heating unit (e.g., chestnut sized anthracite). While some stove and furnace manufacturers list the appropriate fuel type and size, many do not. You may have to rely on the advice of a stove or coal dealer or experienced coal burners using the same unit. If you are not sure about the size, purchase a small test quantity before purchasing in bulk.

Buy good quality coal. A written analysis of the characteristics of the coal you intend to buy may be available from your coal retailer. Even among the high rank anthracites you may have high ash content or low ash fusion temperature.

QUALITY COAL has:

Low ash content. Having less ash means more combustible fuel per unit of volume, less frequent ash removal and disposal, and more heat per dollar spent. Seven to 8% is excellent; 8 - 10% is good; 10-12% fair. Avoid anything over 10% ash content.

Low sulfur content. The lower the sulfur content the better. Sulfur combines with oxygen in the stove to form sulfur dioxide and sulfur trioxide which react with moisture and oxygen in the air to produce an airborne sulfuric acid. It is harmful to humans and vegetation, corrosive to stove pipes and harmful to the strength of mortar in unlined brick chimneys. Sulfur content varies between 0.4 and 5.5%; below 0.6% is satisfactory.

High ash fusion temperature. A high ash fusion temperature minimizes the formation of 'clinkers' or fused ash which can block the grate and increase the amount of labor involved in tending the fire. An ash fusion temperature above 2500°F is preferable and usually obtainable in better quality anthracte.

Low volatile matter. Volatile matter will ignite and be converted to heat only under the proper conditions. If this matter is not oxidized, it will be released as pollutants into the atmosphere.

High fixed carbon content. Fixed carbon is the amount of carbonized residue (coke) which remains after the volatile matter has been driven off. Anthracite is the highest in fixed carbon, in the range of 80 - 98% on an ash-free basis.

QUANTITY

To estimate the amount of coal required per heating season to completely replace your present heating fuel, subtract out the present annual fuel used for cooking and hot water and refer to Table 10.

Prices vary depending on the quality of the coal, the distance from the source of supply, and the means of transportation. Discounts are sometimes available if the coal is purchased well in advance of the heating season. Compare the price of coal between dealers; often there are significant differences.

At cash and carry coal years, there is an approximate 30% savings if the customer bags and transports the coal, or provides the necessary vehicle for hauling bulk coal. Some dealers bag the coal in sizes ranging from 10 to 100 pounds; this convenience will substantially increase the cost. Handling the coal in bags reduces the amount of coal dust and is a convenient unit to move from the storage to the heating unit. An additional fee for home delivery is common; some dealers will not deliver bulk coal in quantities below two tons.

Table 10. Approximate Coal Equivalent of Present Heating Fuel

```
Multiply gallons of No. 2 Fuel Oil by .006 to get
        _____ tons of coal.

Multiply therms of Natural Gas by .0043 to get
        _____ tons of coal.

Multiply kilowatt hours of Electricity by .00023
to get _____ tons of coal.

Multiply cords of air-dried Hardwood by .8 to get
get _____ tons of coal.
```

STORAGE

Coal can be stored indoors or outdoors, but any outside storage should be protected from precipitation, otherwise the coal will freeze together and be difficult to remove. Do not store wet and dry coal together.

A basement storage bin is one of the best storage arrangements. A hinged or sliding door in a window opening facilitates loading by a dump truck with a coal chute. Provide access for delivery trucks within 10′ of the storage. You can expect the inevitable coal dust in the basement, so construct the bin carefully and seal openings.

Coal requires from 33 to 40 cubic feet of storage space per ton. A storage bin 4′ square by 4′ high will hold approximately two tons. Generally more space is allowed so that another delivery can be made before the bin is completely empty.

Figure 26. Coal Storage Bin

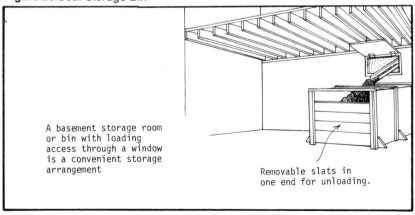

A basement storage room or bin with loading access through a window is a convenient storage arrangement

Removable slats in one end for unloading.

Operating Techniques

GENERAL OPERATING PROCEDURES

Size and Type of Coal

Always follow manufacturer's instructions regarding the type and size of coal to burn, as well as the method of operation. These instructions are usually based on the manufacturer's tests and experience with the type of coal available in the area where the stove was built. Many manufacturers of coal stoves recommend anthracite only. Warranties often do not apply when other types of coal than those recommended are burned. **Do not** burn cannel coal in stoves, furnaces or boilers as the volatile gases may cause dangerous explosions.

Stoves designed for the lower ranks of coal generally have a large firebox and provisions for supplying more secondary air compared to a stove for anthracite giving the same heat output. Furnaces or boilers with stokers are designed to burn either bituminous or anthracite coal and the fuel cannot be switched.

Seasonal Variations

In the spring and fall, it is difficult to maintain a low heat output; either the house will overheat, or the fire may go out and require the tedious process of re-lighting. If the coal stove is used to supplement a central heating system using another fuel, you may choose to operate the coal stove only during the coldest part of the winter.

Another option would be to use wood in the stove during the milder part of winter, but to a lesser extent the same problem of overheating vs low efficiency occurs with wood. If wood will also be burned, the operator must learn different techniques for proper wood combustion, and be aware of creosote problems.

Controlling the Rate of Burn

Do not attempt to decrease the heat output by reducing the amount of coal in the firebox. A deep charge of coal will give even heat and a long fire; it may take several hours before the whole bed is ignited. If the fuelbed is too shallow the primary air will pass too quickly through the fuel and not break into tiny streams of air necessary for proper mixing with coal gases.

Increasing the fuelbed depth, decreasing the size of the coal used, or less frequent ash removal will cut down the air flow and produce a lower heat output when required. It is also important that a coal heater not be filled with excess coal that might block the flue gas exit and cause carbon monoxide to enter the house.

Coal responds slowly to changes in draft settings. When a change in heat output is needed, make a small change in the setting and wait for the temperature to stabilize.

Breaking in a New Stove

Break in new stoves slowly. If possible, light a small initial wood fire in the stove while it is outside, to burn off any oils and their fumes. Once installed, a few wood fires and then a small coal fire will allow the cast iron to cure.

The Overheated Stove

Keep the ashpit door closed, except during the start-up period, or overheating can result. If a stove is left with improper damper settings, usually an excess of primary air, the stove and stovepipe can become red hot and the intense radiation may ignite nearby combustibles. (Figure 27)

Figure 27. The Overheated Stove

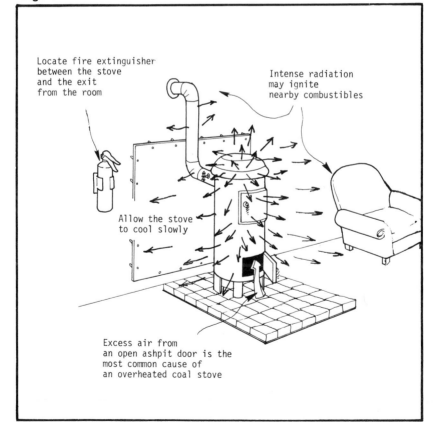

Locate fire extinguisher between the stove and the exit from the room

Intense radiation may ignite nearby combustibles

Allow the stove to cool slowly

Excess air from an open ashpit door is the most common cause of an overheated coal stove

If the stove or stovepipe becomes red hot, adjust the dampers to reduce the air supply, but do not close the dampers completely. Allowing the stove to cool gradually will prevent further damage from thermal stress. **Never** use water to cool the stove as this will increase thermal stress and likely damage the stove irreparably.

Ashes

Always protect the stove grate from direct contact with the fire by a layer of ash 1″-2″ thick to prevent grate overheating and keep unburned coal from dropping through the grate openings.

The single most common problem with coal stove operation is insufficient shaking and ash removal. Shake down the ashes whenever the ash accumulation on the grate is excessive; generally once or twice a day is sufficient. If the ashes build up excessively, they eventually block the grate, inhibit the air flow and put out the fire. If ashes are allowed to accumulate in the ash pan up to the grates, normal cooling of the grates is restricted, which may cause premature failure of the grates.

Figure 28. Ash Removal

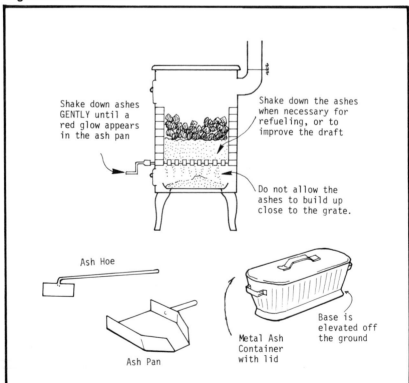

Shake the ashes down **gently**. The objective is to remove the ashes without disturbing the fire. Use a few short strokes and stop when the first red coals appear. Shaking down more than necessary after a long burn, usually in the morning or evening, is a good way to lose a fire through cooling. Also, poking and disturbing the fire tends to promote the formation of clinkers or fused ash, which block the draft, will not burn, and must be removed before refueling.

Remove ashes whenever the ash pan is nearly full. Do not let the pan over-fill so the ashes are touching the grate. Any unburned coal which falls through the grate may be screened out through a piece of 1/4″ or 3/8″ hardware cloth. Store ashes in a metal container with a tight lid and place on a noncombustible floor or on the ground away from combustibles. Hidden embers may be present in the ashes. Coal ash may have minerals detrimental to the soil, so they cannot be used as mulch, soil conditioner or fertilizer as can wood ashes.

Clinkers

Clinkers are hard pieces of fused ash that form in the firebox. They can become large enough to inhibit the air flow and cause the fire to die. Once clinkers are formed, they can be removed only from above the grates.

Clinkers are caused by a variety of conditions, the most important being poor quality coal with excess ash content and/or low ash fusion temperature.

Other causes of clinker formation are: too hot a fire, too shallow or too deep a fuelbed, excess shaking or poking which tends to mix the ash and molten coal, and rapid adjustment of draft from very high to very low setting.

BURNING ANTHRACITE

Establishing the Fire

All coal fires must be initially started from the coals or embers of a wood fire or from charcoal. Wood ignites at 550°F, anthracite at 925°F, so building the fire slowly and patiently will produce the best results. Once the fire is established, the initial fire building need not be repeated for weeks, or even months, if the fire is properly maintained.

Leave a layer of ash on the grate, open the drafts and build a wood fire. The best type of fire results from a mixture of paper, finely split softwood and some hardwoods built carefully with air spaces. After 10-20 minutes, when the fire is burning briskly, add a very thin layer of dry, room temperature coal, being sure to leave visible red spaces between the pieces of coal. Adding the coal too soon, or adding too much coal, could smother the fire. Leave the dampers open until this initial load of coal has definitely ignited and started to glow. When the coal has ignited, blue flames will appear above the bed of coals; this indicates that the volatile gases are being burned with secondary air. (Figure 29)

Figure 29. Establishing an Anthracite Fire

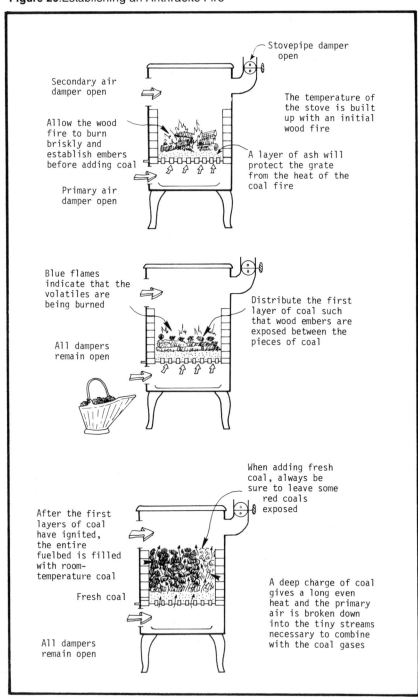

Stovepipe damper
open

Secondary air
damper open

The temperature of
the stove is built
up with an initial
wood fire

Allow the wood
fire to burn
briskly and
establish embers
before adding coal

A layer of ash will
protect the grate
from the heat of the
coal fire

Primary air
damper open

Blue flames
indicate that the
volatiles are
being burned

Distribute the first
layer of coal such
that wood embers are
exposed between the
pieces of coal

All dampers
remain open

When adding fresh
coal, always be
sure to leave some
red coals
exposed

After the first
layers of coal
have ignited,
the entire
fuelbed is filled
with room-
temperature coal

Fresh coal

A deep charge of coal
gives a long even
heat and the primary
air is broken down
into the tiny streams
necessary to combine
with the coal gases

All dampers
remain open

Now add another single layer to the fire and close down the primary air supply to a low-to-medium setting. When a uniform bed of bright coals is distributed across the grate, fill the firebox up to the fire loading door, making sure to leave some red coals exposed to help ignite the gases given off by the new charge. Some people find it easier to build up the fire in 3 or 4 thin layers.

Maintaining the Fire

Once the fire is self-perpetuating, leave the drafts and flue damper only slightly open, to permit slow complete combustion. Anthracite coal has a small percentage of volatile matter. After a few minutes, these volatiles will be released and the coke or fixed carbon that remains requires very little air to burn, so the primary draft and stovepipe damper can be almost closed. Keep the secondary air inlet slightly open to provide oxygen to change carbon monoxide to carbon dioxide. A small blue flame above the coalbed indicates that the volatiles are being combined with oxygen.

Figure 30. Maintaining an Anthracite Fire

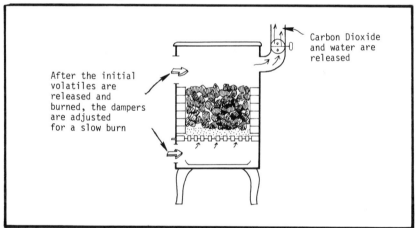

Refueling

If the fire is burning hot and there are several inches of bright coals, a full load of coal can be added. However, if there is not a deep bed, do not shake down the ashes until the fire has been built up with small amounts of coal.

Before opening the fire door, open the dampers to allow the fire to pick up a little and burn off any remaining gases. Check to see if it is necessary to shake down and remove ashes.

When refueling, always leave a portion of the red hot coal exposed on the top.

Scrape some of the red hot coals toward the back and add the new charge of coal to keep the fuel level. In this way, all carbon monoxide and unburned volatile matter from the new coal will be ignited as it passes over the coals.

Fill stoves with hoppers before the coal level drops to the bottom of the hopper. When this is done, no adjustment of the draft controls is necessary.

Preparing the Fire for a Long, Slow Burn

To prepare the fire for an overnight or long burn, shake down and remove excess ashes, and open the drafts to ignite the new charge. Draw the red hot coals to the front of the firebox, and bank or heap the fresh fuel up the sides and back of the stove to cause more gradual burning. Using a smaller size of coal will also reduce the combustion rate by impeding the flow of air. Allow the fresh fuel to establish itself and burn off volatiles, then adjust the dampers for a slow burn. (Figure 31)

Figure 31. Banking the Fire for a Slow Burn

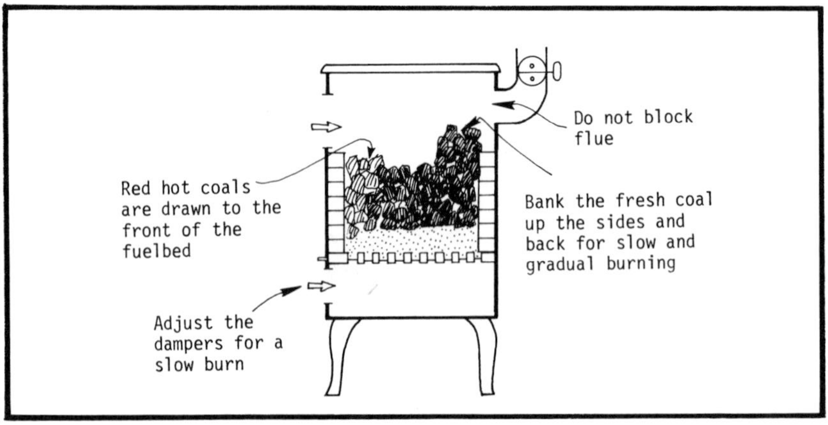

Do not block flue

Red hot coals are drawn to the front of the fuelbed

Bank the fresh coal up the sides and back for slow and gradual burning

Adjust the dampers for a slow burn

Saving a Fire

If the fire has died down after being unattended, it may be necessary to ignite a thin layer of coal before adding a larger quantity. In some cases, it may be necessary to rekindle with wood, before adding coal. This will eliminate the messy and time-consuming procedure of removing all the unburned fuel and starting from scratch. Open the ash door and stovepipe damper and close the fire door damper to get a strong draft through the grate. Do not poke or shake down ashes at this time as this will tend to cool the fire further. Start by adding small amounts of coal. After the fresh coal has ignited and there is a substantial bed of hot coals, the ashes can be shaken down and the dampers adjusted to a lower setting.

If the Fire Goes out

Some stoves are equipped with dumper grates which expel the contents of the stove into the ash pan when desired. The unused coal can be screened out from the ash for reuse. In most cases, however, it will be necessary to remove all the unburned fuel through the firedoor without disturbing the ash layer. Then the fire must be restarted from scratch.

Figure 32. Screen for Coal Recovery from Ashes

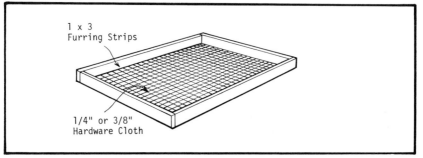

1 x 3
Furring Strips

1/4" or 3/8"
Hardware Cloth

BURNING BITUMINOUS COAL

Bituminous coal burns differently from anthracite, due to its higher volatile content. The first flames will be long, and generally orange or yellow. They will be accompanied by a considerable amount of smoke. As the gases burn off, the flames become shorter and may change color due to the types of impurities present. The flame length also varies with the rate of burn, the longer flames indicating a hotter fire.

Bituminous coal burning involves more maintenance than anthracite. Unless the coal was given a dustless treatment, there will be much more dust in handling. Certain measures, such as an airtight stove with snug-fitting stovepipes and chimney connection, and as little agitation as possible when breaking up caked coal and removing ashes, will lessen the amount of dust that escapes into the house. Greasy dust settles on everything, even vertical surfaces. It can be reduced, but it is difficult to eliminate. Also, more soot will collect on heating surfaces and in pipes, requiring more frequent cleaning.

Low-Volatile Bituminous Coal

Bituminous coal with less than 20% volatile content is generally fired with the conical method. The first fire is built in the same manner as with anthracite. Once the fire is established, add coal to the center of the firebox, forming a cone. More primary air flows around the perimeter when the fuelbed is shallow, creating a hot fire around the cone which drives off the volatiles and allows them to burn. After the volatiles are burned, the coke formed will burn more slowly and you will get a long burn cycle.

Adjust the dampers about the same as for anthracite except allow more secondary air to enter and open the flue damper until the volatiles are burned.

Figure 33. Firing Low-Volatile Bituminous Coal

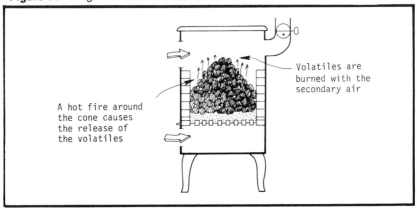

Some coals cake and fuse as they burn and this will eventually block the passage of oxygen through the coals below. Before refueling, **gently** break up the caked bed of coals, being careful not to mix the coal as this will increase the chance of clinker formation. When refueling, always leave some red coals exposed to allow the volatile matter released from the fresh coal to be burned. If the fresh coal covers the hot coals, the gases will be released, but the smothered fuelbed will not be able to ignite them.

Figure 34. Soft coals tend to cake and fuse.

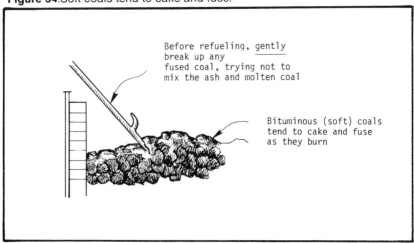

If a flame does not start immediately after firing (because the live coals are not hot enough to ignite the gases), use paper or kindling to start a blaze. Failure to establish a flame after firing bituminous coal is likely to cause a minor explosion or 'puffback.' To achieve maximum efficiency, leave the secondary damper open just enough to avoid puffbacks.

High-Volatile Bituminous Coal

High-volatile coal having more than 20% volatile content ignites easily and burns somewhat like wood with long smoky flames.

One method for starting the fire is to pile fresh coal against the back or side of the firebox, allowing a little to cover the grate area. Paper and kindling are placed against the coal and ignited. This ignites the coal pile from the outside and reduces the number of times that you have to add coal. When recharging, place coal where the kindling was and heat from the burning coal will slowly penetrate the fresh coal allowing for gradual distillation of the volatiles. It is important that any hot coals be removed from the empty half before refueling, leaving just a layer of ash. Otherwise there will be partial burning and a lot of smoke.

Figure 35. Firing High-Volatile Bituminous Coal

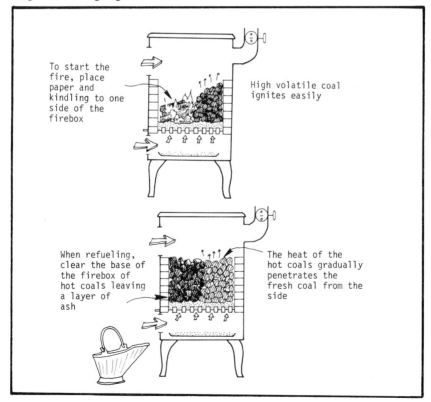

The dampers are regulated the same as with other fuels except that more secondary air is added to burn the volatiles coming off the top of the fire. For overnight operation, shake the fire and add coal. Allow the volatiles to burn off before closing the damper in the fire door and flue. Close the primary air damper to the desired heat level.

APPENDIX A—Cutting
Firewood with a Chainsaw

When any significant amount of wood is to be cut, a chainsaw is often used. Unfortunately chainsaw accidents and injuries are quite common. According to a recent Consumer Product Safety survey, two of every three accidents to casual operators and helpers are **caused by inadvertent contact with the moving chain.** Careless actions, such as reaching across or holding the work near the moving chain, or loss of footing and subsequent loss of saw control, account for many accidents.

Kickback is the major unpredictable chainsaw hazard. Whenever the chain near the upper portion of the nose catches in the wood on an obstruction, it violently jerks the saw back and up. Kickback has caused many serious cuts to the chest and face. Some operators reach into the running chain while struggling to regain balance.

Figure 36. Know the Hazards of Chain Saw Operation

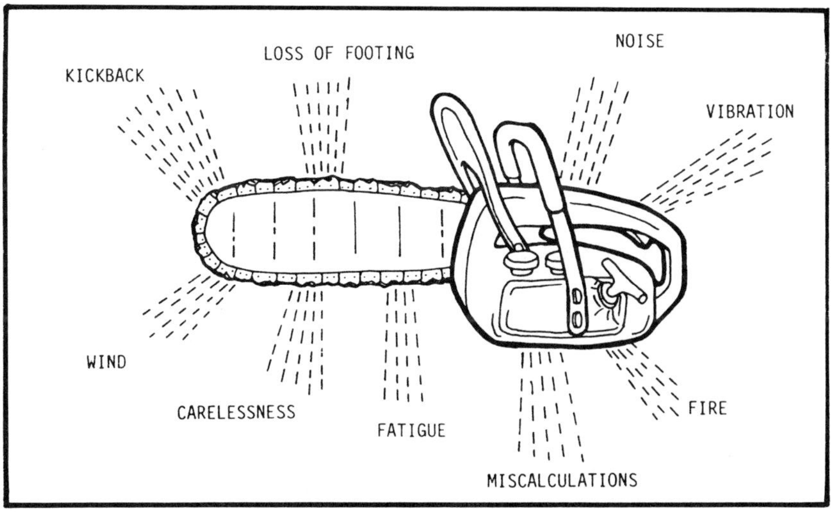

Felling and cutting timber is hard work, so good physical condition is important. An exhausted person can become a potential accident victim so frequent rest breaks are essential.

81

Weather can create very serious hazards when cutting trees. The **wind** can come up suddenly or change direction unexpectedly, causing a tree to fall in the wrong direction. Avoid cutting trees on windy days. Instead, use these days for limbing (removing the limbs from the trunk) or bucking (cutting the trunk into desired lengths). **Rain, snow and ice** may lead to unsafe footing. Rather than risk an injury, postpone work until conditions improve.

Trees that hang up when cut are extremely dangerous. They have hit and killed chainsaw operators as they were cutting the tree off at the stump.

EQUIPMENT

Protect head, ears, feet, eyes and hands with:

- Trim fitting trousers, shirts and jackets to reduce the chance of becoming entangled in the saw. Knee pads fixed in the pants are often used.

- Light non-slip gloves to protect hands from abrasion and woodcuts.

- Footwear with a good grip to prevent falls. Boots help to protect the lower legs. Steel-toe safety boots protect the toes.

- Safety goggles, face shield, or eye glasses with safety lenses to prevent injury from flying wood chips or sticks.

- Protection against the 100 decibel or higher noise level of the saw. **The unprotected user should limit operating time to one hour per day maximum.** Good muffs or comfortable molded plugs will allow a full work day without ear damage.

- A hard hat to prevent serious head injury from falling branches or limbs.

- A chain saw sized to fit the task.

Protect your body with the proper safety equipment when using a chainsaw

OPERATION

- Let the saw do the work. Don't force it through the cut.
- Use the buddy system; don't work alone.
- Hold the saw firmly, with both hands in the proper position when cutting. Make sure the thumbs and fingers completely encircle the saw handle.
- Keep your elbows and knees slightly flexed for maximum control. Do not work with your arms extended.
- Operate the saw to the side of the body so that it will not swing into you if it kicks back or cuts through the wood unexpectedly.
- Never shift hand position or cross arms for easing strain or for better reach without first turning off the saw.
- Never cut over your head.
- Cut with the lower side of the saw as much as possible. This is the safest, least tiring position.
- Keep the guide bar in the middle of the cut so that the cutters on the opposite side will not bind. Do not twist the guide bar.
- Do not allow a running saw to contact the ground or metal; one such contact can dull the chain more than cutting dozens of trees.

Watch for these **kickback causes:**

- Abrupt change of wood characteristics (i.e., green to dry, knots, etc.)
- Running the saw too slowly
- Buildup of damp sawdust
- A twig caught in the chain and jamming against the work
- A branch or obstruction on the opposite side
- Twisting of the saw so that the cutters grab the wood
- Sawing with the point of the guide bar (nose sawing)
- The closing of the kerf or slit cut by the saw.

Kickback is certain under some conditions. Cutting with the upper side of the bar may be convenient but it is dangerous, especially with the larger more powerful saws. Sudden kickback will occur if the chain "locks" in the cut when the saw is used in this position.

Some saws have a chain brake which operates automatically when a sudden reverse of motion of the saw occurs. On most saws this brake is not effective in the horizontal position as when felling a tree. Anti-kickback noseguards are also available for some saws, but they must be removed for deep cuts. Once this guard is removed it is often never replaced.

If you are an inexperienced operator, make trial cuts to become accustomed to cutting and handling characteristics of the saw. **Keep the chain sharp and properly adjusted** so it and the weight of the saw do the cutting. Do not apply extra pressure.

FELLING

Consider the characteristics of each tree when determining the felling direction. A tree may lean or be unbalanced due to uneven top growth or breakage even through the trunk does not lean. Large diameter branches are good indicators of imbalance.

Check for hollow or rotten trees which may fall unpredictably. Be alert for loose branches or "widowmakers" in the tree. Special cutting methods are required to cut leaning trees. These trees may split at the stump and kill or seriously injure the chain saw operator.

Prevailing wind direction affects tree growth and balance while present wind conditions affect fall direction. The inexperienced operator should attempt to fell trees only under conditions which indicate a high degree of certainty as to which way the tree will fall. Plan an escape route before starting.

When felling a relatively straight-standing tree:

- Make a notch or undercut on the side of the tree on which it is expected to fall. It should have a depth of approximately one-third the diameter of the tree. Make the lower notch cut first. This keeps the chain from binding and being pinched by the wedge of wood while the notch cut is made. (Figure 37)

- Make the felling or back cut about 1″ higher than the horizontal cut. The felling cut should be kept parallel with the horizontal notching cut. Do not cut all the way through. Cut it so that wood fibers are left to act as a hinge, keeping the tree from twisting and falling in the wrong direction.

Figure 37. Felling a Tree

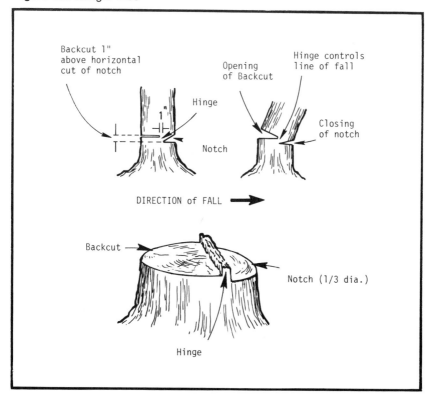

- Keep the guidebar in the middle of the cut so the cutters returning in the top groove don't recut the wood. Don't twist the guidebar in the groove. Guide the saw into the tree—don't force it. The rate of feed will depend on the size and type of timber.

- Remove the saw from the cut before the tree falls. The tree will begin to fall as the felling cut approaches the hinge fibers. Move to a safe spot away from the stump and **look up** for falling branches.

- Do not cut through the hinge fibers. The tree could fall in any direction—maybe in the direction in which you are retreating.

A binding saw and closing kerf indicate an error in judgment. At the first such indication, remove the saw. If the saw cannot be removed, do not struggle with it. Shut off the engine, clear the area and plan a course of action using wedges to remove the saw.

If you are tiring and the saw has not progressed to a near fall, remove the saw, shut it off and rest until you are able to proceed with confidence. Also, **check the fuel supply before** starting a cut which will require a long running period. When you add fuel, always add chain lubricating oil.

A well-balanced tree may have to be wedged to direct a tree fall. Use only wooden, aluminum or plastic wedges—steel or iron wedges may damage the chain. Two wedges rather than one insure a forward fall of the tree. Strike squarely with a sledge or mallet with a face broader than the wedge. Careless or excessive blows may cause the wedge to pop out, swinging the tree backward. **Do not** use an axehead as a wedge or driver because it may break.

The manipulation of fall control comes with experience. Approach complex falls with extreme caution. Above all, do not neglect wind effects. Always keep the felling direction as simple as possible and avoid working on windy days.

Use a tractor or winch to pull away a tree that hangs-up in another tree during felling. A small tree can sometimes be rolled with a lever or peavey to dislodge it. **Do not** cut the standing tree or climb either tree.

LIMBING

Many chainsaw accidents occur during limbing. Using a lightweight saw with a short bar makes holding and maneuvering easier. The lower horsepower helps the operator control the saw in kickback situations. Limbing progresses much more rapidly when the saw is sized to the task.

Cut **limbs** on the top side of the trunk before removing those resting on the ground. Remove **lesser branches** as the work progresses up the trunk, as they impair vision, present obstacles and may cause kickback due to twigs lodging in the blade. Use extra caution when cutting small diameter limbs, as the slender material may catch in the saw and be whipped toward you. Cut branches to desired length before they are cut from the trunk.

Saw limbs on the opposite side of the trunk from where you stand, using the trunk as a barrier. If it is necessary to work with the saw on the same side, keep the saw to the side of the body so that it will not swing into the legs or head. Avoid reaching with the saw and always maintain good footing and balance.

Cut the branches resting on the ground to improve working conditions underfoot as the work progresses. The tree may sag or roll as each branch is cut. **Key branches stabilizing the tree should be left until last.** A closing kerf signals the probability of kickback. Keep the engine speed up—a slow moving saw chain is more likely to lock than one cutting freely at a higher speed.

Final supporting branches might be saved to facilitate bucking. The trunk, however, should be stable and not vulnerable to roll during bucking.

BUCKING

Special hazards of bucking are unexpected roll of logs and kickback. Be sure of your footing when working on hillsides and always work on the uphill side of the log. Raise and check the trunk or roll the log to complete the cut. Do not saw into the ground. Use levers, sturdy poles or bars as much as possible. Do all manual lifting with proper lifting technique to avoid back strain or injury. (Figure 38)

It is usually easier to handle wood in four foot lengths and stack it to dry. Then cut the pieces on a saw buck or pallet rack before use in the fall.

Figure 38. Cutting the Tree into Desired Lengths

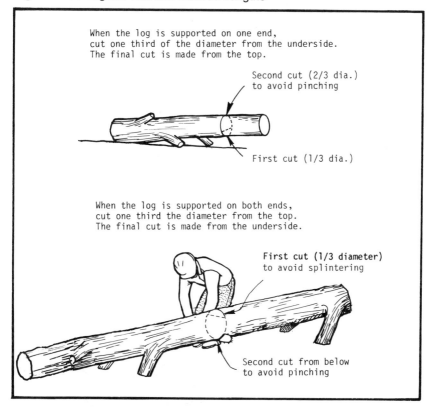

When the log is supported on one end,
cut one third of the diameter from the underside.
The final cut is made from the top.

Second cut (2/3 dia.)
to avoid pinching

First cut (1/3 dia.)

When the log is supported on both ends,
cut one third the diameter from the top.
The final cut is made from the underside.

First cut (1/3 diameter)
to avoid splintering

Second cut from below
to avoid pinching

SPLITTING WOOD

Tools used to split firewood logs include a splitting axe, an eight-pound sledge, a splitting maul and wedges. The axes and wedges should be kept reasonably sharp so keep a file and a stone handy.

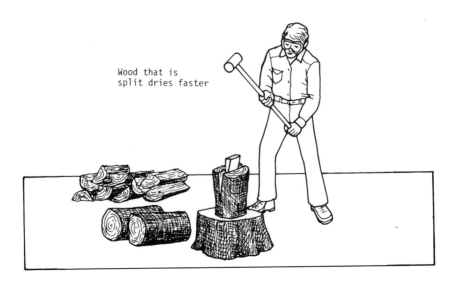

Wood that is
split dries faster

It takes practice to learn to split wood safely and efficiently. Learn to read the flow of the grain and work with this flow rather than against it to make wood splitting more enjoyable. Grain patterns differ between tree species and a straight-grained ash will always split easier than an elm with its interlocking and interweaving wood fibers. The grain also varies within a tree and will prove to be most difficult around branches and knobs.

Never split wood directly on the ground as this is a good way to strike a rock or your foot. Place the piece to be split on a chopping block which can be either a larger log or a stump about 20″ high. Flex your knees when you swing so that the angle between the log and your axe is 90 degrees. If does not split, drive a wedge in at the center; two wedges placed halfway between the center and the edge may be needed with large or stubborn blocks. Wedges carefully placed can also be used to free a buried axe or maul.

A crotched log will help
steady an uneven log
for splitting

When the log has a branch stub or visible knot in it, locate the split line so that the crack will run through the center of the knot or stub. Hidden knots can sometimes be detected by observing a curve in the otherwise straight grain. A crotch log is difficult to split—either saw the legs apart, or stand the log on its legs and drive a wedge in line with the legs' centers.

REFERENCES

Coal—The Complete Hand-Fired Coal Heater Handbook by B. Donatelli. 1980. DRI Publications, Bedford, NH.

Heating with Coal by John Bartok, Jr. 1980. Garden Way Publishing Co.

Standard for Chimneys, Fireplaces, Vents and Solid Fuel Burning Appliances. 1984. ANSI/NFPA 211. National Fire Protection Association, Batteryworth Park, Quincy, MA 02269

Solid Fuel Furnaces and Boilers by John W. Bartok, Jr. 1982. Garden Way Publishing Co., Charlotte, VT 05445. 220 pp. $7.95.

The Wood Burners Encyclopedia by Jay W. Shelton and A. W. Shapiro. 1976. Vermont Crossroads Press, Waitsfield, VT 05673. 155 pp. $6.95.

Solid Fuel Safety Study Manual for Level 1 Solid Fuel Safety Technicians 3rd Ed. 1984. Wood Heating Education and Research Foundation, 1101 Conn. Ave. NW, Suite 700, Washington DC 20036.

Woodheat/85. Energy Publications, Inc., Gilford, NH 03246. Newsstand price $2.95. Available by mail $5.

Wood Heat Safety by Jay W. Shelton. 1979. Garden Way Publishing Co., Charlotte, VT 05445. 165 pp. $8.95.

Wood Stove Operation and Advanced Design to Reduce Emissions of Incomplete Combustion Products by A. C. S. Hayden and R. W. Bratten. Canadian Combustion Research Laboratory, March 1985. CANMET, 555 Booth Street, Ottawa, Canada K1A 0G1.

Wood Smoke Pollution: Is It A Health Risk and How Can It Be Controlled?. Maine Dept. of Human Services.